CIVILISATIONS DU PROCHE-ORIENT

PHILOLOGIE
VOLUME 2

Série dirigée par : F. Vallat

Abbreviation of this volume : *CPOP* 2

© Recherches et Publications
Neuchâtel - Paris
ISSN 1420-7737
ISBN 2-940032-11-4

Printed in Belgium

All rights reserved. No part of this book may be reproduced or translated in any form, by print, photoprint, microfilm, microfiche or any means without written permission from the publisher.

CIVILISATIONS DU PROCHE-ORIENT
PHILOLOGIE
VOLUME 2

Ashkharbek Kalantar

The Mediaeval Inscriptions of Vanstan, Armenia

Prepared for Publication by
Husik Melkonyan and Gagik Sarkissian

Edited by Aram Kalantarian

Translated by V.G. Gurzadyan

Published with the support of the Calouste Gulbenkian Foundation,
the Centre for the Advancement of Archaeological and Historical Research, Geneva,
and Recherches et Publications

Recherches et Publications
1999

Ashkharbek Kalantar in St. Petersburg (c. 1910)

"While Lehmann-Haupt and Marr are often credited with sparking investigations into the history and prehistory of eastern Anatolia and southern Transcaucasia, this compilation* of selected writings and photographs of Ashkharbek Kalantar (1884-1942) makes a persuasive case that it was he who most thoroughly shaped archaeology in the Armenian highlands.

Kalantar's life and work provide a testimony to the enduring importance of the Armenian highlands to world history and prehistory and can, one hopes, stimulate renewed appreciation for not only the region's archaeological record but also its rich intellectual history."

A.T. Smith, *AJA* 100 (1996), 638-639.

---

* A. Kalantar, *Armenia : From the Stone Age to the Middle Ages. Selected Papers* (Ed. by G. Karakhanian), *Civilisations du Proche Orient*, Série 1, vol. 2, Neuchâtel, Paris, 1994.

NATIONAL ACADEMY OF SCIENCES OF ARMENIA
INSTITUTE OF ARCHAEOLOGY AND ETHNOGRAPHY
Scientific Heritage, Volume 1

ASHKHARBEK KALANTAR

THE MEDIAEVAL INSCRIPTIONS OF VANSTAN, ARMENIA

Prepared for Publication by
HUSIK MELKONYAN and GAGIK SARKISSIAN

Edited by ARAM KALANTARIAN

Translated by V.G. GURZADYAN

Published with the support of the Calouste Gulbenkian Foundation,
the Centre for the Advancement of Archaeological and Historical Research, Geneva,
and Recherches et Publications

Recherches et Publications
1999

NATIONAL ACADEMY OF SCIENCES OF ARMENIA
INSTITUTE OF ARCHAEOLOGY AND ETHNOGRAPHY
Scientific Heritage

Editorial Board
G. Grigoryan, S. Harutyunyan,
A. Kalantarian, G. Karakhanian, and D. Vardumian

This first volume of the Series 'Scientific Heritage' has been recommended for publication by the Scientific Council of the Institute of Archaeology and Ethnography of the National Academy of Sciences of Armenia.

It is dedicated to the 1700th anniversary of the adoption of Christianity as the official religion in Armenia.

CONTENTS

PREFACE (A. Kalantarian)	....	IX
BIOGRAPHY OF ASHKHARBEK KALANTAR	....	XI
A. KALANTAR'S PUBLISHED AND UNPUBLISHED WORKS	....	XII
THE INSCRIPTIONS OF VANSTAN (A. Kalantar)	....	1
1. Foreword	....	2
2. Introduction	....	4
3. The Inscriptions of Vanstan (Nos. 1-63)	....	8
4. Inscriptions from the Surroundings of Vanstan (Nos. 64-67)	....	54
5. New Inscriptions from Vanstan (Nos. 68-76) (H. Melkonyan and G. Sarkissian)	....	62
KALANTAR'S STUDIES ON EPIGRAPHY (H. Melkonyan and G. Sarkissian)	....	73
VANSTAN IN THE HISTORICAL CHRONICLES (H. Melkonyan and G. Sarkissian)	....	79
APPENDICES		
I. Preliminary Report on the Trip to Imirzek in 1912 (A. Kalantar)	....	85
II. Report Presented at the Oriental Section of the Imperial Russian Archaeological Society (A. Kalantar)	....	86
III. The Excavations of Prof. N. Marr at Ani in the Summer of 1910 (A. Kalantar)	....	88
GLOSSARY (H. Melkonyan and G. Sarkissian)	....	91
LIST OF PLATES	....	94

PREFACE

Archaeologist and historian Ashkharbek Kalantar (1884-1942) was among the scholars whose fruitful research was interrupted by Stalin's regime of terror. His rich scientific heritage consists of unpublished manuscripts, a unique collection of glass photographic plates, and many other documents; they were confiscated during his arrest in 1938, and the whereabouts of most of these items is still unknown. One of the unpublished manuscripts, which was discovered by chance and is devoted to the description of mediaeval architectural monuments in the vicinity of Ani, the mediaeval capital of Armenia, was published in a recent volume of selected papers by Kalantar.[1] Another manuscript, devoted to the inscriptions uncovered during excavations in 1912 supervised by himself in Vanstan (Imirzek), has fortunately survived in the archive of the Institute of Archaeology and Ethnography of the Armenian National Academy of Sciences. This manuscript was originally prepared for publication in St. Petersburg under the editorship of his teacher Nicholas Marr. Unfortunately, the finished manuscript and many other materials kept in the printing-house of the Russian Academy were damaged during the flood of 1924. Later, in 1935, Kalantar succeeded in resurrecting the manuscript from the surviving materials, but again circumstances did not allow the appearance of the work.

In view of the exceptional historical value of Kalantar's "Inscriptions of Vanstan," the Scientific Council of the Institute of Archaeology and Ethnography has decided to publish the manuscript. It has been prepared for publication by Husik Melkonian and Gagik Sarkissian. In the course of their work, Melkonian and Sarkissian visited the monument and its environs and compared the readings of Kalantar with the surviving inscriptions. It became clear that after the excavations of 1912, the majority of the stones of the monastery had been broken and reused by the Muslim population of the nearby village as building materials for their houses and sheds. Therefore, the great majority of the inscriptions which were studied by Kalantar now have the value of originals. Nine new inscriptions were also found, and these have also been included in this volume.

Kalantar's manuscript is reproduced with very minor changes, since he followed all the principles of scientific epigraphy when he wrote it. Also included herein are the extant original photos, copies of the inscriptions, and Kalantar's readings. Some new photos were made by V. Hakobian, and copies of new inscriptions by L. Avagian. S. Stepanian's measurements of the monument have been used in the redrawings of H. Sarkissian.

To give the reader an idea of Kalantar's multilevel research in epigraphy, including work on prehistoric rock carvings, hieroglyphs, Urartian cuneiform, and mediaeval Armenian, an essay by

---

[1] A. Kalantar, *Armenia: From the Stone Age to the Middle Ages. Selected Papers* (Ed. by G. Karakhanian), *Civilisations du Proche Orient*, Série 1, vol. 2, Neuchâtel, Paris, 1994.

PREFACE

Melkonian and Sarkissian is included in the volume. They have also prepared an account of the role played by the Vanstan monastery in the mediaeval Armenian chronicles.

In addition to the "The Inscriptions of Vanstan" (both in the original Armenian and in English translation), this volume includes two reports by Kalantar on the excavations of 1912,[2] and a report of N. Marr's work at Ani in 1910 [3] where, 26 years old, Kalantar was also associated. Finally, the book includes a list of the scientific papers published by Kalantar, as well as facsimile copies of some documents with notable historical interest. A glossary of personal, geographical and other names is appended to the end of the volume.

We are grateful to the grandson of Kalantar, astrophysicist V.G. Gurzadyan, for the translation and help during the work on this volume.

Aram Kalantarian

---

[2] A. Loris-Kalantar, *Bull. Acad. Impériale des Sciences de St.-Pétersbourg*, Série VI, 7, 127, 1913; *idem, Comm. Imperial Archaeological Society* 22, 1914.

[3] A. Kalantar, *Horizon* 189, 192, 1910.

Biography of Ashkharbek Kalantar

1884, February 11	Ashkharbek Loris-Melik Kalantar born in the village of Ardvin of Armenia, to the ancient *Melik* family of Lori.
1905	Finishes the Nersisian school in Tiflis.
1905-1906	Teaches in schools of Akhaltzkha (Georgia).
1906	Finishes the Gymnasium in Tiflis.
1907	Enters both the Armenian-Georgian-Persian and the Historical-Linguistic Departments of the University of Saint Petersburg; begins contacts with Academician N. Marr. First participation in the Ani Expedition under the directorship of N. Marr.
1911	Finishes the University with honors.
1912	Full member of the Archaeological Institute of Saint Petersburg.
1912	Sent by the Russian Imperial Academy of Sciences to Imirzek (Vanstan) in Armenia.
1912	Sent by the Academy to the Surmalu region (now in Turkey).
1913	Sent by the Academy to the Lori region in Armenia.
1914, March 15	Elected as a member of the Imperial Archaeological Society.
1914	By a resolution of the Russian Academy of Sciences, becomes keeper of the Asiatic Museum of Saint Petersburg.
1914	By a resolution of the Academy becomes the head of the XIIIth Ani Archaeological Excavation campaign.
1917	Participates in the second Van Archaeological Expedition with Prof. N. Adontz.
1918	Organizes the evacuation of about 6000 items from the Ani Museum to Armenia.
1918-1919	Lectures at the Transcaucasian University in Tiflis.
1919	Becomes one of the seven founding members of the newly established University of Erevan.
1919-1932	Permanent member and Scientific Secretary of the Commission of Ancient Monuments.
1920-1938	Member of the teaching staff at the Erevan State University; founds the Chair of Oriental History and Archaeology (1922).
1922-1937	Organizes about 30 expeditions in different regions of Armenia.
1926-1930	Studies the Urartian inscriptions found in Armenia.
1928-1935	Studies rock-carved figures and ancient irrigation systems on Mt. Aragatz and in the Geghama range.
1929	Becomes professor at the Erevan State University.
1931	Head of the Excavations in Old Vagharshapat.
1932	Reports his discoveries at the Archaeological and Ethnographical Conference in Leningrad.
1935	Reports his discoveries at the IIIrd International Iranian Congress in Leningrad.
1938, March 19	Arrested at home and sentenced to death as an "enemy of the nation;" later, the sentence was replaced by jail.
1941, January	Last message received from prison.
1942, June	Approximate date of death in prison in Russia.

A. Kalantar's Published and Unpublished Works

(Titles 1-70 were compiled by A. Kalantar himself)

1. Excavations in Ani, *Horizon*, 1907, July.
2. Excavations by Prof. N. Marr in Ani, *Horizon*, 1909, August.
3. The Question of the 'National Museum', *Hovit*, 1909, and *Gortz* 68, 1909.
4. Ani Archaeological works, *Surhandak* 9, 12, 1909.
5. Excavations by Prof. Marr in Ani in Summer 1910, *Horizon* 189, 192, October, 1910.
6. Lori at the Time of the Korikeans : Cultural-Political Rise of Northern Armenia in the Xth-XIIth Centuries, Candidate thesis (Recommended by N. Marr and the Council of the Oriental Faculty of St. Petersburg University for publication in the series : Texts and Studies in Armenian Philology but has finally not been published. Over 100 pages), 1912.
7. Preliminary Report on the Trip to Imirzek in the Summer of 1912, *Bull. Acad. Impériale des Sciences de St.-Pétersbourg*, Série VI, vol. 7, 127, 1913 ; *Mél. asiat.* 16, 1, 1914.
8. Preliminary Report on the Trip to Lori in the Summer of 1913, *Bull. Acad. Impériale des Sciences de St.-Pétersbourg*, Série VI, vol. 7, 775, 1913 ; *Mél. asiat.* 16, 105, 1914.
9. The Basilica in Zor and the Ruins of an Ancient Caravanserai, *Khristiansky Vostok* 3, 101, 1914.
10. The Word 'qayq', *Khristiansky Vostok* 2 and other short articles in *Khristiansky Vostok*, 1912-1914.
11. Imirzek — The Excavations and Descriptions of the Monuments (scheduled to appear in the Series *Bibliotheca Armeno-Georgica*, edited by N. Marr, but the publication was cancelled due to the damage of the materials in the 1924 flood in St. Petersburg).
12. *Armenian Inscriptions of Imirzek*, 1916 (unpublished).
13. *Armenian and Georgian Inscriptions of Kobayr and on the Chalcedonianism in Northern Armenia*, 1916 (unpublished).
14. *Political Parties in Armenia before the Rise of the Bagratides* (B.A. Thesis), 1916.
15. The Destruction of Ancient Monuments in the Region of Military Operations at the Turkish Front-Line, *Horizon*, 1915.
16. *The Description of Armenian Manuscripts in the Caucasian Museum — Muraviev Collection of the Asian Museum* (the manuscript should have been published by the Caucasian Museum in the beginning of 1916 but was cancelled due to wartime conditions ; it was recovered and submitted for publication to the Institute of Oriental Studies of the Russian Academy of Sciences) (unpublished).
17. *Hittites* (over 80 pages) ; report at the Meeting of the Historical Philological Faculty of Transcaucasian University, 1918 (unpublished).

18. *Archaeology*, Part I. Textbook based on lectures given at the Armenian University, 86 pages, 1923, Erevan.
19. The Protection of Ancient Monuments in Armenia and Forthcoming Problems in Archaeology, *Verelk* 2 and 3, 1923.
20. On the Report by Academician N. Marr in Erevan, *Soviet Armenia* 145, 1924.
21. Stone Age in Armenia, *Nork* 4 and 5, 207, 1925; partly translated in French in *Revue des Etudes Arméniennes*, 1927, 271-296, and in English, along with reports by Marr, Lehmann-Haupt, Belk, Reinach (*Revue Archéologique* 7, 1928, XI-XII). See also M. Boul (*L'anthropologie* XXXVIII, notes 5-6), 1929, F. Nansen (*Betrogenes*, 1928, 232-234, 244), A. Goetze (*Kulturgeschichte des Alten Orients*, 1933, 47).
22. An Important Archaeological Find, *Soviet Armenia* 25, 1925.
23. Archaeological News, *Soviet Armenia* 51, 1925.
24. Palaeolithic Remains in Armenia, *Soviet Armenia* 65, 1925.
25. Archaeological Studies in Armenia in the Past, *Soviet Armenia* 214, 1925.
26. Artists in Soviet Armenia: A.I. Tamanian, *Soviet Armenia* 132, 1926.
27. Archaeological Survey of Sevan, *Soviet Armenia* 221, 1926.
28. Avan Stone-Mine as a Neolitic Dwelling, *Erevan* 221, Paris, 1926.
29. Armenian Commission of Ancient Monuments, *Rahviran* 3, 1926.
30. Academy of Sciences and Armenology, *Bull. of Institute of Sciences of Armenia* 1, 1926.
31. How well are we understood? (On the Foreign Armenian Press), *Soviet Armenia* 35, 1927.
32. What Can we Learn by Studying Ancient Armenian Architecture? *Arvest* 3, 4, 1927 (reprinted in several foreign Armenian magazines).
33. Two Cuneiform Inscriptions of Rusa, Son of Sardur (Nor-Bajazet and Odzaberd Inscriptions), *Bull. of Commission of Ancient Monuments* 3, 1927.
34. Igeroglifici scaperti in Armenia, *Le Orfane Armene* 5, Torino, 1927.
35. Inscriptions d'Arménie en caractères inconnus, *Revue Archéologique* 30, 43, 1929.
36. A New Chaldean Cuneiform Inscription from the Village of Janfida, *Bull. of the Commission of Ancient Monuments* 4, 1930.
37. Commission of Ancient Monuments and Archaeological Studies in Armenia, *Science and Research Work in Armenia in 1920-1930*, NKP Publ., p. 88-100, Erevan, 1931.
38. *Excavations in Old Vagharshapat*, Erevan, 1935.
39. An Ancient Irrigation System in Soviet Armenia, *Bull. Inst. History and Literature* 2, Erevan, 1933.
40. Irrigation Systems and the Cult of Water in Ancient Armenia (unpublished).
41. New Facts about the Antiquity of Erevan, *Soviet Armenia* 232, 1933; reprinted in *Nok* 10, 11, Paris, 1933.
42. Armenian Inscriptions of Ayrivank, *Corpus of Armenian Inscriptions* 1 (unpublished).
43. *Vanstan*, 1933 (to be published by the Institute of History and Literature).
44. *Aragatz in History*, Erevan, 1935.
45. Discovery of a Pre-Chaldean Dwelling near Leninakan, *Soviet Armenia* 115, 1934.
46. The Excavations of an Ancient Town near Leninakan, *Communist* 4, 1934.

47. Discovery of a Pre-Chaldean Dwelling near Leninakan in Soviet Armenia, *Problems of the History of Pre-capitalist Society*, GAIMK 9, 10, Leningrad-Moscow, 1934.
48. 58 articles for the Armenian Encyclopaedia, 1934-1935.
49. The Irrigation System in Ancient Armenia and Problems of Stock-Breeding, *Soviet Armenia*, 1935.
50. An Attempt at the Reconstruction of Armenian History ; report on session in the Erevan State University, February, 1935.
51. *The Irrigation System of the Epoch of the Vishaps in Armenia*, 1935 (unpublished).
52. Academician N. Marr, *Harvatzain Usanogh* 19, 1935.
53. *Armenian Epigraphic Data and their Role as a Source of History* (unpublished).
54. The Hunt Theme in Armenian and Iranian Art. Paper delivered at the plenary session of the IIIrd International Congress on Iranian Art, 16-X-1935, Leningrad, 1935.
55. On the Scientific Role of the Byurakan Monument, *Prolet. Tourist* 2-3, 1935.
56. Monuments of Material Culture in Soviet Armenia, *Moscow Daily News* 10, 1935.
57. *Armenia in the Archaic Period of its History, Materials on Armenian History* (Megalithic Culture, Hieroglyphs, etc.), over 300 pages (unpublished).

Manuscripts Ready for Publication or in Preparation

58. *History of the Ancient Orient*, university textbook, over 200 pages.
59. *Armenian History* (Ancient Period), textbook.
60. *Archaeological Studies in Armenia During the Last 15 Years.*
61. *The Palaeolithic in Armenia — The 'Tzitzernakaberd Man'*, (Collective work ; Geology : O. Ayvazian ; Anthropology : V.N. Vishnevsky ; Archaeology : A. Kalantar).
62. *The Historical and Archaeological Content of the Erevan Katoghike Church*, 1937.
63. *Garni — Epigraphic Monuments*, 1937.
64. *The Epoch of Shota Rustaveli*, 1937.
65. Report on S. Barkhudarian, *Chaldean-Urartian State*, 1934.
66. Report on S. Barkhudarian, *Inscriptions of Geghard*, 1934.
67. Critics and discussion of H. Manvelian, *The Dissolution of Armenian Feudalism in the XIIIth-XIVth centuries and the Political-Economic Strengthening of the Spiritual Class*, 1935.
68-69. Critique and Report on two works : Thesis and course by T. Vanyan on the History of the Ancient World.
70. Report on A. Harutyunian, *On Peasant Revolts in Armenia in the Early XVIIth Century.*

Addendum

71. The Yezidis, their Life and Religion, 1912 (unpublished).
72. Inscriptions of Dega Angelica in Odzun in the XIIIth century and their Role in the Study of the Historical Grammar of the Lori Dialect, 1913 (unpublished).
73. On the Trip to Erevan State, *Bull. Oriental Dept. of Imper. Archaeol. Society* 22, p. IX, 1914.

A. KALANTAR'S PUBLISHED AND UNPUBLISHED WORKS

74. The Insignia of the City of Ani as a Reflection of Antiquity, 1917 (unpublished).
75. The Symbolic Construction of the Armenian Cross-Stone — Khachkar, 1917 (unpublished).
76. On the Dating of the Odzun Basilica, 1917 (unpublished).
77. Architectural Monuments of Shirak : Khtzkonk, Tekor, Bagaran, Agarak, Tzpni, (Notebook of Expedition), 1920 ; published in No. 83] and partly in Nos. 81 and 82.
78. Catacomb-type Burials in Haghtz, *Erevan University Bulletin*, 1925 (unpublished).
79. Lori, Lalvar - Etymological Interpretation, *Erevan University Bulletin*, 1925 (unpublished).
80. A Rare Find in Armenia, *Inform. Bulletin VOKS* 9-10, II-III, 1927.

Later Works and Publications
81. Agarak, *Caucasus and Byzantium* 2, p. 143, Armenian Acad. Sc. Publ., 1980.
82. Tzpni, *Caucasus and Byzantium* 3, p. 178, Armenian Acad. Sc. Publ., 1982.

    Nos. 81 and 82 were prepared for publication by P. Mouradian.
83. *Armenia : From the Stone Age to the Middle Ages. Selected Papers* (Ed. by G. Karakhanian), (= *Civilisations du Proche Orient*, Série 1, vol. 2), Neuchâtel, Paris, 1994.

Facsimile copy of a page of Kalantar's manuscript on Vanstan.

Pl. I

1

2

3

Pl. II

4

5

6

Pl. III

7

8

9

Pl. IV

10

11

12

13

Document established by the Russian Museum of Emperor Alexander III, St. Petersburg (May 10, 1912), giving A. Kalantar authority "to begin ethnographical investigations and to study ancient monuments in the states of Tiflis and Erevan, and in the district of Kars." (Archive of Matenadaran, Erevan)

МИНИСТЕРСТВО ИМПЕРАТОРСКАГО ДВОРА.

ИМПЕРАТОРСКАЯ АРХЕОЛОГИЧЕСКАЯ КОММИССІЯ.

22 Мая 1914 г.

№ 1122

С.-Петербургъ.

Зданіе ИМПЕРАТОРСКАГО Зимняго Дворца.

Открытый листъ.

На 1914 /четырнадцатый/ годъ.

Выданъ этотъ листъ Члену-сотруднику ИМПЕРАТОРСКАГО Русскаго Археологическаго Общества Ашхаръ-Беку Андреевичу Лорисъ-Калантару Императорскою Археологическою Коммиссіею на право производства археологическихъ раскопокъ въ теченіе 1914 года на земляхъ казенныхъ, общественныхъ и принадлежащихъ разнымъ установленіямъ въ предѣлахъ городища Ани и его окрестностей Карсской области.

съ обязательствомъ доставить въ Коммиссію отчетъ или дневникъ по произведеннымъ раскопкамъ, а также, при особой описи всѣхъ находокъ, наиболѣе цѣнные и интересные изъ найденныхъ предметовъ для представленія ихъ на Высочайшее Государя Императора воззрѣніе.

Предсѣдатель Императорской Археологической Коммиссіи,
Гофмейстеръ Двора ЕГО ВЕЛИЧЕСТВА, Членъ Государственнаго Совѣта

Дѣлопроизводитель

Листъ этотъ дѣйствителенъ на одинъ годъ и, по минованіи надобности, долженъ быть

Document established by the Imperial Archaeological Society (May 22, 1914), giving A. Kalantar the permission to coordinate the archaeological campaigns at the site of Ani and in the district of Kars.

Императорская
АКАДЕМІЯ НАУКЪ.

Непремѣнный Секретарь.

„5" ноября 1914 г.

№ 3627.

Петроградъ.

УДОСТОВѢРЕНІЕ.

ИМПЕРАТОРСКАЯ Академія Наукъ симъ удостовѣряетъ, что предъявитель сего, окончившій курсъ факультета восточныхъ языковъ ИМПЕРАТОРСКАГО Петроградскаго Университета, дѣйствительный членъ ИМПЕРАТОРСКАГО Петроградскаго Археологическаго Института и членъ-сотрудникъ ИМПЕРАТОРСКАГО Русскаго Археологическаго Общества Ашхарбекъ Агалоевичъ | Андреевичъ | Лорисъ Калантаръ | Калантаровъ | былъ командированъ ИМПЕРАТОРСКОЮ Академіею Наукъ лѣтомъ текущаго года съ научною цѣлью на Кавказъ для полной регистраціи памятниковъ въ г. Ани, Карсской области, и его окрестностяхъ и производства археологическихъ раскопокъ въ указанномъ районѣ, и что А.А. Лорисъ-Калантаромъ собранъ весьма важный научный матеріалъ, приведеніемъ коего въ порядокъ онъ занятъ въ настоящее время для представленія Академіи матеріаловъ и отчета о произведенныхъ во время Анійской археологической кампаніи подъ руководствомъ его, А.А. Лорисъ-Калантара, научныхъ работахъ, составленіе какового отчета займетъ приблизительно шесть мѣсяцевъ.

За Непремѣннаго Секретаря,
Ординарный Академикъ, Тайный Совѣтникъ

Правитель Канцеляріи Конференціи

Document established by the Imperial Academy of Sciences, St. Petersburg (November 5, 1914), stating the importance of the results obtained during the XIIIth archaeological campaign at Ani which was coordinated by A. Kalantar.

ՀԱՅՈՑ ԱԶԳԱՅԻՆ
ԽՈՐՀՈՒՐԴ

АРМЯНСКІЙ НАЦІОНАЛЬНЫЙ
СОВѢТЪ

«28» Марта 1918 г.
№ 1736

АШХАРЪ - БЕКУ
ЛОРИСЪ - МЕЛИКЪ - КАЛАНТАРУ

Армянскій Національный Совѣтъ уполномачиваетъ Васъ принять всѣ необходимыя мѣры къ эвакуаціи изъ А н и всего имущества, представляющаго исторически-археологическую цѣнность, въ селеніе С а н а и н ъ или А х п а т ъ Лорійскаго участка и къ сохраненію ихъ въ полной безопасности, при чемъ въ дѣлѣ размѣщенія этихъ цѣнностей и охранѣ ихъ В ы имѣете дѣйствовать съ Уполномоченнымъ Армянскаго Національнаго Совѣта, Ованесомъ Фаддѣевичемъ Т у м а н я н ц е м ъ.

Предсѣдатель Совѣта [signature]

Членъ-Секретарь [signature]

Resolution of the Chair of the Armenian National Assembly (March 28, 1918) appointing A. Kalantar for the organization of the evacuation of the archaeological finds from Ani.

XX

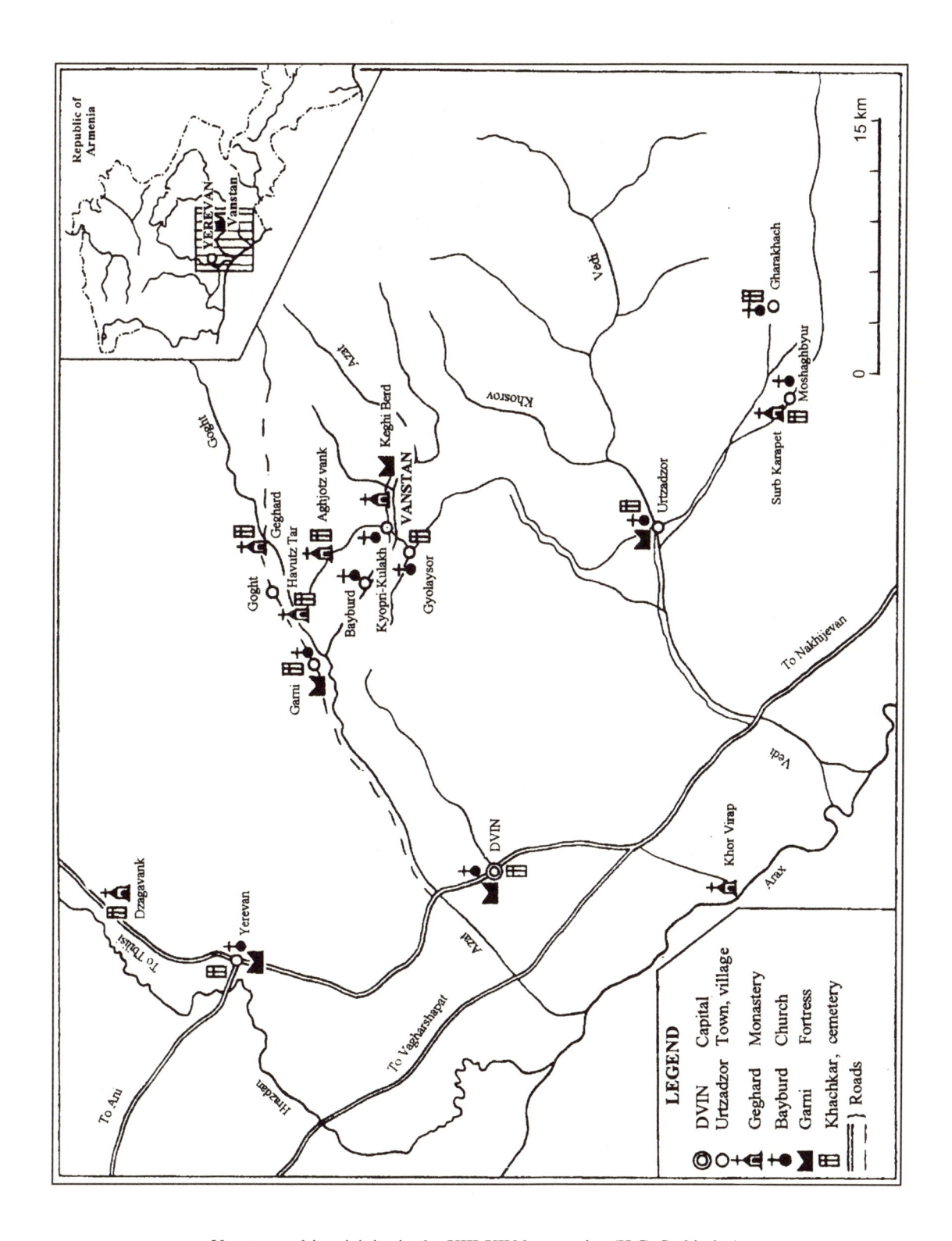

Vanstan and its vicinity in the XIII-XIVth centuries (H.G. Sarkissian).

THE INSCRIPTIONS OF VANSTAN

by Ashkharbek Kalantar

(Original text in Armenian and English translation)

1. FOREWORD

The study of the inscriptions of Vanstan (Imirzek), along with the excavation of the monument and its investigation, were undertaken by us in accordance with the recommendation of the Imperial Academy of Sciences (see the Preliminary Report on the Trip to Vanstan in the Bull. Acad. Impériale des Sciences de St.-Pétersbourg, 1913, p. 127-130).

The majority of the inscriptions studied during 1916-1917 were prepared for publication by the Academy in a special volume in the series "Bibliotheca Armeno-Georgica", under the editorship of Academician N. Marr. However, because of my absence due to the blockade of the roads upon my return from the second Van expedition in 1917, which made it impossible to journey to Petrograd, the publication was delayed until 1924, when the flood damaged all the materials.

Using the 37 surviving original prints, I have now recovered the manuscript on the inscriptions of Vanstan for publication.

I request all those who will deal with this manuscript to handle the pictures with extreme care, since they are the only surviving copies.

Ashkharbek Kalantar (31.12.1935)

1. Երկու խոսք

Վանստանի (Իմիրզեկ) արձանագրությունների ընթերցումը ինչպես նաև նրա ամբողջ հուշարձանի պեղումներն ու ուսումնասիրությունը կատարված է մեր կողմից Կայսերական Գիտությունների Ակադեմիայի հանձնարարությամբ ու գործուղումով՝ (Предварительный отчет о поездке в Имирзек, Известия Императорской Академии Наук, 1913, стр., 127-130):

Այդ աշխատանքների արդյունքից մեզ այժմ հետաքրքրող արձանագրությունների մասը 1916-1917 թթ. տպագրվում էր Ակադեմիայի կողմից և կազմելու էր Ակադեմիական Bibliotheca Armeno-Georgica սերիայի մի հատորը, ակադ. Ն.Մառի խմբագրությամբ։ Սակայն իմ բացակայության պատճառով (1917 թվի աշնանը Վանի 2-րդ հնագիտական արշավախմբից անկարելի եղավ Պետրոգրադ վերադառնալ՝ ճանապարհների փակման պատճառով), տպագրությունը ձգձգվեց, մինչև որ 1924 թվին տեղի ունեցած ջրհեղեղի ժամանակ ոչնչացման տպարանում ամբողջ շարվածքը և կլիշեները, շատ ուրիշ գործերի հետ միասին։

Միակ մնացորդներն այդ աշխատությունից սրագրումի 37 արտատպությունն է կլիշեներից, որի օգնությամբ ես այժմ պատրաստեցի Վանստանի արձանագրությունները տպագրության համար։

Խնդրվում է բոլոր նրանց, ովքեր ձեռքի տակ կունենան այս գործը՝ մեծ խնամքով վերաբերվեն դեպի նկարները, քանի որ դրանք եզակի օրինակներ են, որոնցից պատրաստվել են կլիշեներ։

Աշխ.Քալանթար (31.12.1935 թ.)

2. INTRODUCTION

Vanstan is the historical name of the site uncovered by the excavations. The present village (i.e. in 1912, H.M., G.S.) is called Imirzek (with a Turkish population). It is located in the Garni region, in Mili canyon, along the upper course of the river Azat. The ruins in the village are the remnants of the lower parts of the walls of a church built upon a rock. For this reason, inscribed fragments of the monument are scattered around the vicinity and over the slope in an easterly and southerly direction down to the very bottom of the canyon.

Very few of the wall fragments remained *in situ*. Most had been reused by the villagers to construct their various buildings. Even the ruined monument itself had been reused as a cattle shed.

During excavations, the monument was cleaned and opened, as was the area located to the north and west. The simple constructions erected on the ruins were removed, and the fragments that were scattered over their environs were collected within the church.

The fragments that were discovered in the course of the excavations are very numerous, and represent essential architectural pieces, bas-reliefs, sculptures and processed stones covered with inscriptions. They were dug out of the soil, but they were also found in the vicinity of the church, in various areas of the slope, and even at the bottom of the small and large southern and eastern canyons. Other stones were extracted from the walls of village houses and cattle sheds. Its plan (Pl. 17) — an elongated quadrangle, with four wall cavities and a dome — is remarkable, not because of its dimensions, but because of its fine exterior. According to the inscriptions, it was built in the early XIIIth century. This is confirmed by the peculiarities of its style and the multitude and diversity of its inscriptions (Pl. 1-14, 20-23), an expression of the XIIIth-century renaissance of Armenian art. The monument was built completely of basalt.

The inscriptions were collected and read by us as thoroughly and exhaustively as possible. Missing fragments of several damaged inscriptions seem to be lost forever. The number of inscriptions found was 63, in addition to 4 from the surrounding area, for a total of 67.[1]

The majority of the inscriptions are from the XIII-XIVth centuries. Those of later epochs are purely of funerary type. Only two inscriptions (from the surrounding area) are from the Xth century. No inscription daing to later than the XVIth century was found.

As to their content, the inscriptions include building commemorations, benefactions and memorials, with the exception of one that has the character of a decree (No. 67 from Kyopri-Kulakh[2]).

---

[1] Investigation of the site in 1996 showed that only 28 of the inscriptions discovered by A. Kalantar have survived. However, 9 new inscriptions were found then, and these are published at the end of this manuscript.

[2] A mediaeval site near Vanstan where ruins of a one-nave basilica and of other early Christian monuments are located.

2. Առաջաբանի տեղ

Վանստանի կոչումը պեղումների հետևանքով արձանագրություններից պարզված տեղի պատմական անունն է: Ներկայիս (1912 թ, Հ.Մ., Գ.Ս.) գյուղը կոչվում է Իմիրզեկ (թուրք բնակչությամբ): Սա գտնվում է Գառնիի շրջանում, Մելի ձորում, Ազատ գետի վերին հոսանքներում: Գյուղում եղած հուշարձանի ավերակները in situ պահպանված մի եկեղեցու պատերի ստորին հատվածներն են, որոնք ևստած են մի ապառաժի վրա՝ ձորաբերանում. այդ իսկ պատճառով ընկած ճարտարապետական մասերը և արձանագրությունները ոչ միայն փռվել են հատակի վրա, նրա պատերի տակ և բակում, այլ սփռվել են հուշարձանի արևելյան և հարավային ուղղությամբ ամբողջ լանջի ու զառիվայրի վրա՝ դեպի ձորը և անգամ գլորվելով հասել են մինչև նրա խորքերը:

Շուրջն ընկած մասերից շատ քչերն են մնացել իրենց տեղերում և հողով ծածկվել, նրանց մեծ մասն օգտագործվել է տեղացիների կողմից իբրև շինանյութ իրենց շինարարական կարիքների համար: Ավերված հուշարձանն անգամ ազատ չի մնացել, նրա վրա և անմիջապես կից շինված են մի քանի հարդանոցներ, գոմեր ու կալեր:

Պեղումներն ամբողջովին մաքրեցին ու բաց արին հուշարձանը և նրա հյուսիսային ու արևմտյան կողմից շրջապատող հրապարակը, որ հանգստարան է հիշատակված: Ավերակների վրա կառուցված նոր հասարակ շենքերը վերացվեցին, պահպանելով սակայն նրանց արտաքին պատերը, դարձնելով այն շրջապարիսպ ավերակների համար, որի ներսում, եկեղեցու արևմտյան պատի առաջ և անմիջապես տաճարի տեղում տեղափոխվեցին ու դասավորվեցին այս ու այն գտնված բեկորները:

Պեղումներով երևան հանված մնացորդները շատ մեծ թիվ են կազմում, սրանք ճարտարապետական կարևոր մասեր են, բարձրաքանդակներ, քանդակազարդ ու արձանագրված քարեր: Հանվել են նրանք հողի տակից, տաճարի շրջակայքից, լանջի զանազան մասերից և նույնիսկ հարավային և արևելյան կողմերի փոքր ու մեծ ձորերի խորքերից: Այս քարերի մի մասն էլ հանված է գյուղացիների մարագների, գոմերի ու տների պատերից: Եկեղեցին ըստ իր պլանի (աղ. 17) (երկարացած քառանկյունի, պատերին կպած չորս որմնամույթերով, գմբեթահար) աչքի է ընկել ոչ իր խոշորությամբ, այլ իր հարուստ գեղարվեստական արտաքինով: Ըստ արձանագրական տվյալների, այն կառուցվել է XIII դարի սկզբում, որը հաստատվում է միանգամայն իր տիպական ու ոճական առանձնահատկություններով, արձանագրությունների, քանդակների և բարձրաքանդակների շատությամբ ու բազմազանությամբ՝ իբրև բնորոշ արտահայտություն XIII դարի հայ արվեստի նոր վերածնության ու ծաղկման դարաշրջանի (աղ. 1-14, 20-23): Կառուցված է ամբողջապես բազալտից:

Արձանագրությունները հավաքվել ու մանրակրկիտ պրպտումներով կարդացվել են սպառիչ կերպով, որքան հաջողվել է մեզ դա անել: Մի քանի եղծված արձանագրությունների պակասող մասերն ըստ երևույթին ոչնչացված են բոլորովին: Հուշարձանին վերաբերող գտնված արձանագրությունների թիվն է 63, և 4 արձանագրություն շրջակայքից, ընդամենը 67 հատ[1]:

Արձանագրությունների մեծամասնությունը XIII և XIV դարերի են. ավելի ուշ գրվածները զուտ դամբարանային են. միայն երկու արձանագրություն (շրջակայքից) X դարի են պատկանում: XVI դարուց ավելի ուշ արձանագրություն չգտնվեց:

---

[1] 1996 թ. տեղում կատարված ուսումնասիրություններով պարզվեց, որ Աշխ.Քալանթարի հայտնաբերած արձանագրություններից պահպանվել են 28-ը, որոնց մի մասը հատվածաբար: Հայտնաբերվել է 9 նոր արձանագրություն, որը նպատակահարմար գտանք ներկայացնել հեղինակի աշխատության վերջում:

Besides their historical, economical, social and linguistic importance (dialect, original words, names of sites, etc.), the inscriptions of Imirzek hold great archaeological interest, especially due to the frequent use in them of monograms, including some novel types. None of the inscriptions has been published previously. The manuscript contains 266 pages, 67 inscriptions, 67 pictures.[3]

---

[3] The expedition of the Moscow Imperial Archaeological Society directed by V.M. Sisoev in 1907-1908 had gathered a few inscriptions, which were later published by K.H. Kuchuk-Hovhanissian, *Materials on Archaeology of the Caucasus* 13, p. 67-70, Moscow, 1913.

Իրենց բովանդակությամբ արձանագրությունները շինարարական են, նվիրատվական և հիշատակագրային, բացի մեկից, որը հրովարտակային բովանդակություն ունի (համար 67 - Քյուֆրի Կուլախ)².

Բացի պատմական, տնտեսական, կենցաղային ու լեզվական (բարբառային ձևեր, բոլորովին նոր տերմիններ, նոր տեղանուններ և այլն) նշանակությունից, Իմիրզեկի արձանագրությունները ներկայացնում են հնագրական մեծ հետաքրքրություն, մանավանդ փակագրերի հաճախակի գործածությամբ, որոնց մեջ պատահում են և բոլորովին նոր ձևեր: Վանստանի արձանագրություններից և ոչ մեկը հրատարակված չէ մինչև այժմ³ (այս աշխատության մեջ՝ 266 թերթ, 67 արձանագրություն, 67 նկար):

---

² Միջնադարյան գյուղատեղ Վանստանի մերձակայքում, ուր պահպանվել են միանավ բազիլիկ եկեղեցու ավերակները և վաղ քրիստոնեական կոթողներ:

³ 1907-08 թթ. Մոսկովյան Կայսերական հնագիտական ընկերության արշավախումբը Վ.Մ.Սիսոևի ղեկավարությամբ Վանստանից հավաքել է մի քանի արձանագրություն, որոնք հրատարակել է անվանի հայագետ, Մոսկվայի Լազարյան ճեմարանի պրոֆեսոր Ք.Հ.Քուչուկ-Հովհաննիսյանը (Материалы по археологии Кавказа, Т. 13. Москва, 1913, стр. 67-70):

3. THE INSCRIPTIONS OF VANSTAN

1. *The inscription of the construction*

Situated near the entrance, it covers the upper part of the entrance arch, the timpanum and both of its sides.

(a) From the upper arch only three fragments survived. One bears the inscription ԳՐԻԳՈՐՈ ԹՈՌՆ ՀԱ, and is currently located in a new wall, below the southern rock, below the road, near the cattle shed. Only the backside of the stone is seen, with a special sign indicating the continuation of the inscription from its front to the inner side. The other two fragments with the inscription ՁԵԿԵՂԵՑԻՍ ԵԻ ԸՆԾ were extracted in the course of excavations conducted in various areas of the southern slope. We brought these two fragments into the church and placed them on the carved table-stones.

(b) The timpanum was excavated on the southern slope, not far from the mosque. Its edges are broken. Its present dimensions are: height, 1.16 m, length, 1.57 m. It was not possible to move the timpanum up to the church.

(c) The right-hand side of the entrance lay inside the church; part of it was visible even before our excavations.

(d) The left-hand side of the entrance (and many other architectural fragments) has been reused by the villagers. We removed it to the church and put it near the western wall. In its present condition, its length is 2.25 m, the width of the inner side is 1 m, and its opposite side is 0.85 m.

The arch of the entrance and its two sides are shaped of two similar semi-cylinders, with inscriptions on their flat areas. The timpanum is covered by three fine crosses, in one row, the middle one larger than the other two. The inscription continues on the inner side of the timpanum. The sizes of the inscriptions on the various stones are different: on the arch they have 9 cm length, on the timpanum 6 cm, on the sides 11 cm (right), and 10.5 cm (left). The inscriptions are read in the following sequence.

On the timpanum: ՏՐ ԱԾ ՅՍ ՔՍ, 1 on the timpanum, 3 on the first row of the right side, 2 on the upper row of the timpanum, 4 on the left side, 2/2 on the second row of the timpanum, 3/2 on the second row of the right side, written above (on the continuation of the first row), due to the shortage of space.

Expanding the abbreviations and the notations used,[4] and also restoring as far as possible the missing parts, the inscription (middle of the timpanum) reads as follows:

---

[4] Honors or titles.

3. Վանստանի արձանագրությունները

1. Շինության արձանագրությունը

Եկեղեցու մուտքի վրա։ Այս արձանագրությունը բռնել է մուտքը շուրջանակի՝ մուտքի վերին կամարը, տիմպանը (բարավորը - Հ.Մ., Գ.Ս.) և երկու կողերը։

ա. Վերին կամարից պահպանվել են միայն երեք բեկորներ. սրանցից մեկը, որի վրա փորագրված է ԳՐԻԳՈՐՈ ԹՈՌՆ ՀԱ բառակապակցությունը, ներկայումս գտնվում է մի չոր շարվածքի (պատի) մեջ, հարավային ապառաժի ներքևում, ճանապարհի տակ, կալի մոտ։ Երևում է միայն քարի եռևնի մասը, որն ունի հատուկ կանգ՝ փոխադրության համար. քարի երեսը արձանագրության ներսի կողմն է դարձած։ Մյուս երկու բեկորները՝ ՋԵԿԵՂԵՅԻՍ ԵԻ ԸՆԾ մակագրությամբ, պեղումներով հանված են հարավային լանջի տարբեր կետերից։ Այս երկու կտորները փոխադրել ենք եկեղեցու մեջ, ուր նրանք դրված են սեղանի քանդակազարդ քարերի վրա։

բ. Բարավորը պեղված է հարավային լանջի վրա, մզկիթից ոչ հեռու։ Նրա ծայրերը կոտրված են։ Իր ներկա վիճակում հավասար է. բարձրությունը՝ 1,16 մ, լայնությունը՝ 1,57 մ։ Բարավորը չհաջողվեց վերև հանել, տեղափոխել եկեղեցու մոտ։

գ. Մուտքի աջ կողը ընկած է եկեղեցում. նրա մի մասը երևում էր նույնիսկ միջն պեղումները։

դ. Մուտքի ձախ կողը ուրիշ բազմաթիվ ճարտարապետական մասերի թվում օգտագործված էր իմիրզեկցիների կողմից. մենք տեղափոխեցինք եկեղեցի և դրինք նրա արևմտյան պատի մոտ։ Իր ներկա դրությամբ նրա երկարությունը 2,25 մ է, երեսի կողմի ընդհանուր լայնքը՝ 1 մ, իսկ հակառակ կողմից՝ 0, 85 մ։

Մուտքի կամարը և երկու կողերն արտաքուստ մշակված են միանման կիսա-գլանաններով, որոնց հարթ միջնամասերում տեղավորված է արձանագրությունը։ Բարավորը քանդակված է երեք նուրբ խաչերով՝ մի շարքի, որոնցից միջինն ավելի մեծ է մյուսներից։ Արձանագրության շարունակությունը բարավորի քարի վրա է, նրա ներքևի եզերքով։ Առանձին քարերի գրերն իրենց չափերով իրարից տարբերվում են։ Կամարի գրերի երկարությունը՝ 9 սմ, բարավորինը՝ 11 սմ, կողերինը՝ 11 սմ (աջը) և 10,5 սմ (ձախը)։ Արձանագրությունը կարդացվում է հետևյալ հաջորդականությամբ։

Բարավորի վերին մասում կարդացվում է՝ $\overline{SP}$ $\overline{Ա\check{O}}$ $\overline{3U}$ $\overline{\mathcal{L}U}$, ապա 1՝ կամար, + 3՝ աջ կողի առաջին տողը, + 2՝ բարավորի վերին տողը, + 4՝ ձախ կողը, + 2/2 բարավորի երկրորդ տողը, + 3/2 աջ կողի երկրորդ տողը, որի վերջը տեղի սղության պատճառով՝ գրվել է վերևում, առաջին տողի շարունակության վրա։

Լրացնելով կրճատումները և բանալով ծղպատները[4], ինչպես նաև հնարավորության չափով վերականգնելով հենց այն և այլ արձանագրությունների տվյալների հիման վրա՝ արձանագրության չպահպանված, կորած մասերը, արձանագրությունը կարդացվում է այսպես։

(*բարավորի մեջտեղում*) -

---

4   Ծղպատ – պատվի նշան։

Pl. 1:1-3, 2:1-2

2. *The inscription of David, Head of the Ararat State*

On a large stone (2.15 x 0.69 m), broken into two equal parts, is found the inscription of David, "Head of the Ararat State". The fragments of this stone were uncovered by excavation, one to the right of the church, and the other to the north, on the slope. Both parts were removed to the western wall of the church. The inscription has 7 lines; the size of the letters is 7.05 cm.

Expanding the abbreviations, opening the notations and reconstructing the broken parts or damaged letters, we read as shown on p. 11.

ՏԵՐ ԱՍՏՈՒԱԾ ՅԻՍՈՒՍ ՔՐԻՍՏՈՍ

(1) ⌈ԵՍ ՏԵՐ ԴԱԻԻԹ ՈՐԴԻ Գ⌉ՐԻԳՈՐՈ ԹՈՌՆ ՀԱ⌈ՍՍԱՏԻՆԻ ՇԻՆԵՑԻ
Զ⌉ԵԿԵՂԵՑԻՍ ԵԻ ԸՆԾ⌈ԱՅԵՑԻ...

(3) ... Մ ԲԱԶՈՒՄ ԾՆՈՂՔ ԻՄ ԵՂԲԱՐ

(2) ՔՍ ԵԻ ԵՍ ԵՒ ՍՊԱՍԱՈՐՔՍ ՍՈՐԱ ԴԱԻԻԹ ԵՎ ԱՅԼՔՍ ԳՐԵՑԻՆ ։Ի։

(4) ԱԻՐ ԺԱՄ ։Դ։ ԳՐԻԳՈՐՈ Վ⌈ԱՐԴԱ(2/2) ՎԱՌ(ԻՆ), ։Դ⌉։ ԱՂՈՒՏԻՆ ԱԾԱԾ(ՆԻՆ),
։Դ։ ՀԱՍԱՍՏԻՆԻ ՍՈՒՐԲ ԽԱՉ(ԻՆ) ։Գ։..... (3/2) ..... Ա ։Ե։ ԽԱԼԹԻ
ՉԱՏԿԻ(Ն)։ ՈՎ ԽԱՓԱՆԷ ՄԵՐ ՄԵՂԱՅՆ ՊԱՐՏԱԿԱՆ Է ԵԻ ԱՆ (3 հավելյալ)
ԵԾՍ ԱՌՅԷ։

2. *Արարատյան նահանգի առաջնորդ Դավիթի արձանագրությունը*

Մի խոշոր ու մասիվ քարի վրա (2,15 x 0,69 մ), որ կեսում կոտրված է երկու մասի, գտնվում է «Արարատյան նահանգի առաջնորդ» Դավիթի արձանագրությունը։

Արձանագրված քարի մասերը հանված են պեղումներով, մեկը եկեղեցու հյուսիսային կողմում՝ կալի մեջ, իսկ մյուսը՝ հարավային կողմում՝ լանջի տակ, երկուսն էլ տեղափոխված են և դրված եկեղեցու արևմտյան պատի տակ։ Արձանագրությունը՝ 7 տող, գրերի երկարությունը՝ 7,05 սմ։

Լրացնելով կրճատումները, բանալով ծպատները և վերականգնելով արձանագրության տարբեր մասերում ջարդված ու եղծված գրերը, արձանագրությունը կարդացվում է այսպես.

ՍՄՅՐԱՆԻԱՅԻԱԼ   Ժ՛ԼԹԼ ․ԻԻԱՆԵԻ․
ԵՍՌԶԱՂՐ՚ԵԹԱՈՒ   ․․․ԻՄՍ ․ԱՍԵՍԴ․
ՆԱՅԱՆԿԻՇԻՆԵՑԻՉԸ   ՈՈՇԿԵՆԻՎԻՐԱՊՆԵ
ՀԱՆԱԿԱՊԵՅԻՈՑԴԶՄՍՄԻՆԱՇՆԵՑԻ՚Ր
Ն՚ԻՈՒՆՇԱՆԻ․ԸՆՏԱԵՅԻԽՍՉՈՈՒՎԵՐԻՉ
Ե՛Ճ․ԳՐՈՒՏՈՐԽ՞ ՓԱՆԻԻ․+ ՉՆԱՉՈՌՈ
ԵԳՐԵՑԻՉԼԵԱԳՄԴ   ՇԻ՚ԸԱԳՐԱԳՄԱԳԵԼՉԲ

Pl. 2:3 and 3:1

Comments: In the first line of the inscription after the letters ԱՅ the letter Ի is seen; in the fifth line after the words ԸՆԾԱԵՑԻ Ի ՍԱ, one can read ՁԴՈՒՆԱ ՎԵՐԻ ԱՅԳԻՆ; then as in the text. (H.M., G.S.)

3. *The inscription of David, builder of the church*

This inscription was engraved on a round pillar, with both edges broken. The fragment was excavated on the north-western slope, above the road. The present length of the pillar is 1.10 m. The inscription has 6 lines, 4 of which are readable, the size of letters is 6 cm.

ԿԱՆԵ ԱՅ
ԵՍՏՐ ԴԵ
ՇԻՆՈՂՄ
ԺԺՆՍԵՏ
ՎՐԻԽ Ր

---

[5] Ivaneh mentioned in the inscription was a noted political and military figure in the Georgian palace, of the Zakarian prince dynasty. He and his brother, amirspasalar Zakaria, freed Armenia from Seljuk Turks in the late XIIth and early XIIIth centuries.

[6] Ter David was the founder of the Vanstan church and its first religious leader.

[7] Khor Virap mentioned in the inscription is a religious centre on the river Arax, at Artashat, the capital of ancient Armenia. According to legend, the Armenian king Trdat III, at the end of the IIIrd century A.D., had imprisoned Grigor the Illuminator, whose efforts later led to the official adoption of Christianity in the Armenian kingdom.

[8] Believed to be a piece of the cross of Christ, and hence one of most sacred religious relics in Armenia.

[9] Dvin, the mediaeval capital of Armenia, is mentioned; Dvin Ter David offered to the Vanstan church his garden situated near Dvin.

ԸՍՏ ՀՐԱՄԱՆԻ Ա(ՍՏՈՒԾՈ)Յ ԺԱՄ⌐ՆԱԿԻ ԱԹ⌐ՆԱՊԱ⌐Կ⌐ ԻՎԱՆԷԻ⁵/
ԵՍ ՄԵՂԱՊԱՐՏՍ ԴԱՒԻԹ⁶, ԱՌՄ⌐ՋՆՈՐԴ ԱՐԱՐԱՏԵԱՆ/
ՆԱՀԱՆԳԻ, ՇԻՆԵՑԻ ՋՍՈՒՐԲ ⌐ԿԱԹ⌐ՈՂԻԿԷՆ Ի ՎԻՐԱՊԻՆ⁷ ԵՒ/
⌐ՇՈՒՐՋԱՆԱԿԻ ՊԱՐՍՊԵՑԻ. ՆՈՅ⌐ՆՊԷ⌐Ս ՋԱՇԱԾԻՆՍ ՇԻՆԵՑԻ ԱԹ⌐ՈՌՍ⌐/
ՀԱՅՈՒՆՑ ՍՈՒՐԲ ՆՇԱՆԻ⁸: ԵՒ ԸՆԾԱԵՑԻ Ի ՍԱ ՋԴՈՒՆԱՎ⁹ ԵՐԻՒ ⌐ՀՈՂ⌐/
ԵՒ ։Ճ։ ԳՐՈՒԻ ՀՈՂ Ի ՋԱՓԱՐԱՆԻՔՆ, ԵՒ ՋՆԱԽԱՉՈՐՈ Հ⌐ՈՂՆ⌐/
ԵՒ ԳՐԵՑԻ ՋԱՒԱԳ ԽՈՐԱՆԻՆ ՇԱԲԱԹ ԱՒՐՆ ՊԱՏԱՐԱԳԵԼ ՋՔՐԻՍՏՈՍ։

Նկատողություն

Արձանագրության առաջին տողում ԱՅ բառից հետո չի նկատվել Ի տառը, հինգերորդ տողում ԸՆԾԱԵՑԻ Ի ՍԱ բառերից հետո վերծանվում է ՋԴՈՒՆԱ ՎԵՐԻ ԱՅԳԻՆ, այնուհետև ինչպես տեքստում (Հ.Մ., Գ.Ս.):

3. *Եկեղեցին շինող տեր Դավիթի արձանագրությունը*՝ կլոր սյունի վրա, որի երկու ծայրերը կոտրված են: Սյունի այս կոտորը պեղված է եկեղեցու հյուսիս-արևմտյան լանջի վրա, ճանապարհի գլխին: Սյունի երկարությունն իր ներկա դրությամբ հավասար է 1,10մ: Արձանագրությունը՝ ընդամենը 6 տող, որից կարդացվում է չորսը. գրերի երկարությունը՝ 6սմ.

ԿԱՄԱՒՆ ԱՅ /
ԵՍ ՏԷՐ ԴԱՒ⌐ԻԹ⌐/
ՇԻՆՈՂ ՍՈՒՐԲ/
ԱԾԱԾՆԻՍ, ԵՏ/⌐ՈՒ⌐
Վ⌐ԻՐԻ Խ⌐Ո⌐Ր ……:

---

[5] Հանրահայտ քաղաքական և ռազմական գործիչ վրաց արքունիքում, Զաքարյան իշխանական տան ներկայացուցիչ։ Իր եղբոր Զաքարիա ամիրսպասալարի հետ XII դարի վերջում և XIII դարի սկզբում Հայաստանը ազատագրել է թուրք-սելջուկներից։

[6] Տեր Դավիթը Վանստանի վանքի հիմնադիրն է և առաջին վանահայրը։

[7] Հռչակավոր վանական կենտրոն Արաքս գետի ձախ ափին, հին Հայաստանի Արտաշատ մայրաքաղաքի տեղում։ Համաձայն ավանդության մ.թ. III դարի վերջում Հայոց Արշակունի Տրդատ Գ արքայի հրամանով այստեղ է բանտարկվել Գրիգոր Լուսավորիչը, որի ջանքերով 301 թ. Հայաստանում պետականորեն ընդունվեց քրիստոնեությունը։

[8] Քրիստոսի խաչելության խաչափայտի բեկոր, որը Հայաստանի ամենանշանավոր սուրբ մասունքներից էր։

[9] Հիշատակված է միջնադարյան Հայաստանի մայրաքաղաք Դվինը, որի մոտ գտնվող այգին Տեր Դավիթը ընծայել է Վանստանի վանքին։

4. Stone found to the north of the church

This stone is now placed on the table inside the church. A few large letters from an unknown inscription are preserved; the height of the letters is 13 cm. Only the following was readable:

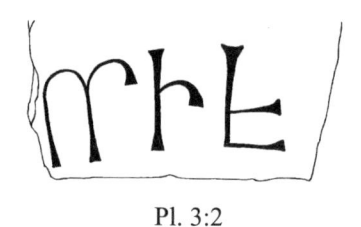

Pl. 3:2

5-6. The gift inscriptions of Kook and Noratung

These were found on a stone (1.20 x 0.74 m) excavated in the church area. The inscriptions, when put together, contain 8 lines. The second line is a continuation of the last line of the first inscription and is written in smaller letters. The first (left) edge of the stone is broken, and therefore the first and second letters of all the lines are missing. Reconstructing the missing parts, we read the inscriptions as shown on p. 15.

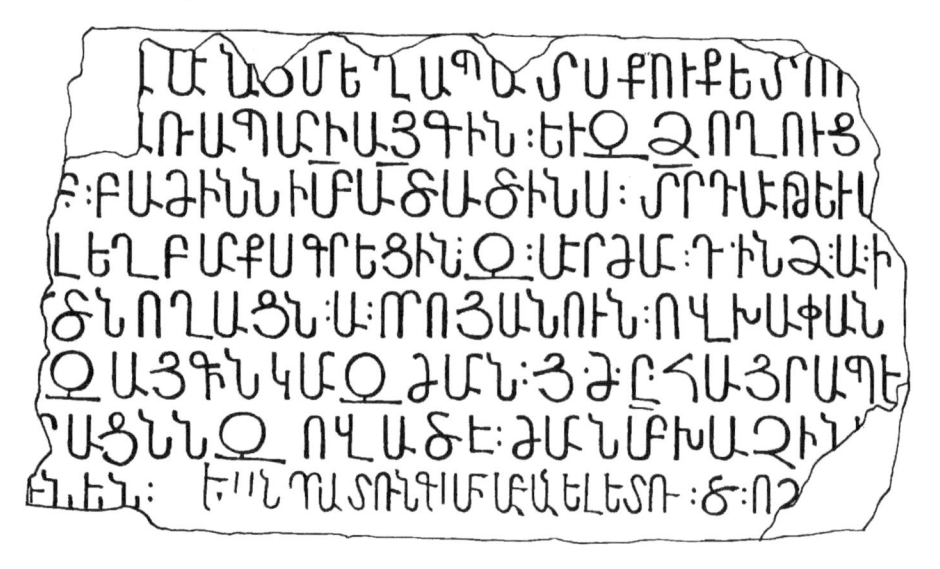

Pl. 3:3

7. Damaged inscription of 1237

The last two lines of an unidentified inscription were found on the upper part of an elongated stone (1.89 x 0.74 m). The stone was extracted from a simple new wall and removed to the western wall of the church. The upper edge of the stone is broken, so that the last line, which was written close to the edge, is almost completely destroyed. The size of the letters is 8 cm.

---

[10] The inscription contains a rare Armenian word (ԱՌԱՊԱՐ) which means a stony site (H. Ajaryan, *Dictionary of Armenian Roots* 1, Erevan, p. 251, 1971).

[11] One can clearly read Ծ(50) on the original photo by Kalantar.

4. Մի քարի վրա, որ գտնվել է հյուսիսային կողմում և այժմ դրված է եկեղեցու սեղանի վրա, պահպանվել է մի քանի տառ անհայտ, խոշորագիր արձանագրությունից, գրերի երկարությունը՝ 13 սմ. կարդացվում է միայն.

... ՈՐԻ Է

5-6. *Քուչի և Նորատունգի նվիրատվական արձանագրությունները* մի քառանկյունի քարի վրա (1,20 x 0,74 մ), որ բացվեց եկեղեցու տեղում: Երկու արձանագրությունը միասին ութ տող են: Երկրորդը կազմում է առաջին արձանագրության վերջին տողի շարունակությունը և գրված է ավելի փոքրացրած գրերով: Քարի առաջին (ձախ) ծայրը ջարդոտված է, ուստի և անհետացել են արձանագրության բոլոր տողերի սկզբի մեկ-երկու գրերը: Վերականգնելով պակասող գրերը՝ տողերի ծայրերում, արձանագրությունը կարդացվում է այսպես.

⌈ԿԱ⌉ՆԱՆ ԱՅ ՄԵՂԱՊԱՐՏՍ ՔՈՒՔ ԵՏՈՒ/
⌈ԻՄ⌉ ԱՌԱՊԱՐԻ[10] ԱՅԳԻՆ ԵՒ ՋՉՈՂՈՒՅ/
⌈:Բ⌉: ԲԱԺԻՆՆ Ի ՍՈՒՐԲ ԱԾԱԾԻՆՍ. ՏԷՐ ԴԱՒԻԹ ԵՒ ⌈Ա/Յ⌉Լ
ԵՂԲԱՐՔՍ ԳՐԵՑԻՆ :Ջ: ԱՒՐ ԺԱՄ , :Դ: ԻՆՉ, :Ա: Ի⌈/Մ⌉
ԾՆՈՂԱՅՆ, :Ա: ՈՐՈՅ ԱՆՈՒՆ: ՈՎ ԽԱՓԱՆ ⌈Է⌉
ՋԱՅԳԻՆ ԿԱՄ ՋԺԱՄՆ :Յ.Ժ.Ք. ՀԱՅՐԱՊԵ/ՏԱՅՆ
ՆՉՈՎԱԾ Է. ԺԱՄՆ ՍՈՒՐԲ ԽԱՉԻՆ ⌈Ա/Ռ⌉ՆԵՆ:
ԵՍ ՆՈՐԱՏՈՒՆԳՍ ՄԻԱԲԱՆԵԼ ԵՏՈՒ : Ժ[11]: ՈՉ⌈ԽԱՐ⌉.

7. *1237 թվի եղծված արձանագրություն*

Երկարավուն քարի վրա (1,89 x 0,74 մ), վերին մասում մնացել է մի անհայտ արձանագրության վերջին երկու տողերը: Քարը հանված է նոր, հասարակ շարվածքի միջից և տեղափոխված ու դրված է եկեղեցու արևմտյան պատի մոտ: Քարի վերին եզերքը ջարդոտված է, ուստի և վերջին տողը, որ գրված է եզերքին շատ մոտ՝ վնասվել է համարյա ամբողջությամբ: Գրերի երկարությունը՝ 8 սմ.

---

[10] «Քարուտ կամ դժվարուստ տեղ» (Հ.Աճառյան, Հայերեն արմատական բառարան, հտ. 1, Երևան, 1971, էջ 251):

[11] Պահպանված լուսանկարի վրա թիվը հստակ կարդացվում է Ծ(50):

l. 3:4

8. *The inscription of atapak and amirspasalar Sadun (1278)*

This inscription is written on two quadrangle stones, which were originally situated close to one another in a wall. The larger of the two was excavated below the southern rock, inside a cattle shed; we removed it to the rock. The other stone (0.60 x 0.55 m) was found above the same rock, close to the southern wall of the church; it was placed back in the church, in front of the table. The initial location of stones within the church is approximate. Presumably they were situated in the southern wall. The inscription has 6 lines, the size of letters is 7 cm. The edges of the first stone are broken, so that the initial and final one or two letters of all the lines are damaged. Since there is room for only two letters (in the fifth line), one has to read ՅԱՌԱՋՆՈՔ and not ՅԱՌԱՋՆՈՐԴՈՒԹԵԱՆ. Restoring the damaged letters, the inscription reads as shown on p. 17.

Pl. 4:1

Comments: The name in the third line of the inscription should be read as ՀԱԽՈՐՍԻՆ, as in the second text. At the end of the fourth line and beginning of the fifth ՅԱՌԱՋՆՈՐԴՈՒԹԵԱՆ is legible. (H.M., G.S.)

---

[12] The prince of the Mahkanaberd region of Armenia, the 'amira' of the city of Tiflis, the commander of the joint Armenian-Georgian army in the seventh and eighth decades of the XIIIth century.

[13] The inscription mentions Grigor Vardapet, the head of the Khor Virap and Vanstan monasteries.

.....ԱՆ ՅԻՇԱՏ⌈Ա⌉ԿԱՑ ԿԱՏԱՐԻՉՔՆ ԱՒՐՀՆԻՆ ՅԱՅ. ԹՎ. : ՈՂՉ : (1237 թվ.)

8. *Աբատակ և ամիրսպասալար Սադունի արձանագրությունը (1278 թ.)*

Գրված է երկու քառանկյունի քարերի վրա, որոնք հուշարձանի պատի մեջ եղել են մի շարքում, կողք-կողքի: Սրանցից մեկը (ավելի մեծը) պեղված է եկեղեցու հարավային կողմի ժայռի ներքևում՝ կալի մեջ և տեղափոխված է ու դրված ժայռի մոտ՝ ճանապարհից վերև, իսկ մյուսը (0,60 x 0,55 մ) գտնվեց նույն ժայռի վերևում՝ եկեղեցու հարավային պատի ուղղությամբ և տեղափոխված է ու դրված եկեղեցու մեջ՝ սեղանի բարձրության առաջ: Քարերի ընկած տեղերը և անգամ արձանագրության գտնված տեղը եկեղեցու շենքի մեջ՝ մոտավոր է: Հավանաբար զետեղված է եղել եկեղեցու հարավային պատի վրա: Արձանագրությունը ունի 6 տող, գրերի երկարությունը 7 սմ:

Արձանագրության առաջին քարի ծայրերը ջարդոտվել են, փշացել բոլոր տողերի առաջին և վերջին մեկ-երկու գրերը: Հինգերորդ տողի սկզբում կա միայն երկու գրի տեղ, ուստի և պետք է կարդալ ՅԱՌԱՋՆՈՔ և ոչ ՅԱՌԱՋՆՈՐԴՈՒԹԵԱՆ:

Վերականգնելով տողերի ծայրերին փշացած գրերը, արձանագրությունը կարդացվում է այսպես.

⌈ԵՍ⌉ ԱԹԱՊԱԿ ԵՒ ԱՄԻՐՍՊԱՍԱԼ⌈ԱՐ⌉ Ս⌈Ա⌉ԴՈՒՆՍ[12] ՏՎԻ / ⌈:Բ:⌉ ՉԱՂԱՅԱՅՏԵՂ ՅԵՐԻՑԱՔԱՇԻՆ :Բ: ԱՌՈՒՈՎ ԵՒ /⌈ՍԱ⌉ԻԳՆ, ՉՈՐ ԵՍ ՀՈԴՈՐՍԻՆ ԷԻ ՏՈՒԵԼ. Հ⌈Ա⌉ԽՈՐՍԻՆ ՈՐ/ԵՐԲ ԱՆԻ ԱՃԱՇՆԻՆ ԷՐԵՏ: Ի ԹՎԻ⌈Ն⌉ : ՉԻԷ: ՅԱՌԱ/⌈ՋՆ⌉ՈՒԹԵԱՆ ԳՐԻԳՈՐ Վ(ԱՐ)Դ(ԱՊԵՏ)ԻՍ[13]. ՈՎ ԽԱՓԱՆ⌈Ի⌉ ՅԻՆՈՑ ԿԱՄ Յ/⌈ԱԻ⌉ՏԱՐԱՑ ԴԱՏԻ ՅԱ(ՍՏՈՒԾՈ)Յ:

Նկատողություն

Արձանագրության երրորդ տողում անձնանունը պետք է կարդալ ՀԱԽՈՐՍԻՆ, ինչպես շարունակության մեջ: Չորրորդ տողի վերջում և հինգերորդ տողի սկզբում վերծանվում է ՅԱՌԱՋՆՈՐԴՈՒԹԵԱՆ (Հ.Մ., Գ.Ս.):

---

[12] Հյուսիսային Հայաստանի Մահկանաբերդի գավառի մեծ իշխան, Թիֆլիզ քաղաքի «ամիրա», հայոց և վրաց զորքերի ընդհանուր հրամանատար (XIII դարի 70-80-ական թթ.):

[13] Խոր Վիրապ և Վանստանի վանքերի առաջնորդ:

9. *The second inscription of atapak and amirspasalar Sadun (?)*

The inscription is found on an elongated quadrangle stone, which was removed to the western wall of the church. The inscription is incomplete: the initial parts of the lines are missing, and were presumably engraved on the adjacent stone to the left, since the edge of the first stone has survived. The upper edge of the stone is damaged, and as a result the first line is totally lost. A few crosses are engraved in a row on the stone. The inscription probably belongs to amirspasalar Sadun: the first letters of his name have survived. The inscription contains 5 lines. Reconstructing the text as much as possible, we read as shown on p. 19.

Pl. 4:2

10. *The 1283 inscription of Grigor vardapet (priest)*

This text is inscribed on a massive quadrangle stone (1.86 x 0.67 x 0.33 m) with a double semicircular sculpture at one end. The stone was excavated below the southern slope, and was removed to a place near the western wall of the church. The inscription is incomplete. The missing parts (6-10 letters in each line) were presumably written on the adjacent stone to the right, which we failed to find. The inscription contains 6 lines (with a small addendum between the third and fourth lines) and is written with great care and in fine letters. The size of the letters is 7 cm. Except for the missing parts, the inscription has survived in rather good condition. Restoring the broken portions, we read:

9. Աբաղակ և ամիրսպասալար Սադունի (?) երկրորդ արձանագրությունը

Արձանագրությունը գտնվում է մի քառանկյունի երկարավուն քարի վրա, հանված ու դրված է եկեղեցու արևմտյան պատի տակ: Պակասավոր է. բացակայում է նրա տողերի սկզբի մասը, որ ըստ երևույթին եղել է հարևան (ձախ կողքից) քարի վրա, քանի որ քարի եզերքն ամբողջ է մնացել: Վնասված է քարի վերին եզերքը, որի պատճառով համարյա ամբողջովին ոչնչացել է արձանագրության առաջին տողը: Քարի վրա, արձանագրության տակ, մի շարքով փորագրված են մի քանի խաչանշաններ: Արձանագրությունը, ըստ երևույթին պատկանում է ամիրսպասալար Սադունին, որի անվան առաջին երկու գրերն են միայն մնացել: Արձանագրությունը հինգ տողից է:

Վերականգնելով, ըստ հնարավորության, արձանագրության պակասող մասերը, կարդացվում է.

⌈ՅԱՌԱՋՆՈՐԴՈՒԹԵԱ⌉Ն (?) ԳՐ (ԳՐԻԳՈՐ) ՎԴԻՆ (ՎԱՐԴԱՊԵՏԻՆ)
ԵՍ/..... ՂԱ ԱԹԱԲԱԿ ԵՒ ՍՊԱՍԱԼԱՐ ՍԱ/⌈ԴՈՒՆՍ ՄԻ⌉ԲԱՆԵՑԱՅ
ՍՈՒՐԲ ՈՒԽՏԻՍ ԵՒ ԵՏՈՒ :Ի: ԴՀ (ԴԱՀԵԿԱՆ) : /⌈ԵՒ ԳԼԽ⌉ԱՒՈՐՔՍ
ԵՏՈՒՆ Ի ՏԱՐԻՆ :Ա: ԱԻ ՊԱՏԱՐ/⌈ԱԳ Ի ՏԱՒ⌉ՆԻ ՍՈՒՐԲ ՍԱՐԳՍԻՆ:

10. Առաջնորդ Գրիգոր վարդապետի 1283 թվի արձանագրությունը գրված է քառանկյունի մասիվ սալաքարի վրա (երկ.՝ 1,86 մ, բարձր.՝ 0,67 մ, հաստ.՝ 0, 33 մ), որի մի ծայրը վերջանում է զույգ կիսաշրջան քանդակներով:

Քարը պեղված է հարավային լանջի տակ և տեղափոխված եկեղեցու արևմտյան պատի մոտ: Արձանագրությունը պակասավոր է, տողերի ծայրերի պակասող մասերը, (6-10-ը գիր յուրաքանչյուր տողում) ըստ երևույթին, գրված է եղել հարևան (աջ կողմից) քարի վրա, որ մեզ չհաջողվեց գտնել: Արձանագրությունը բաղկացած է վեց տողից (ունի փոքրիկ հավելում 3-4-րդ տողերի միջև) գրված է մեծ վարպետությամբ և ոճավոր գրերով, գրերի երկարությունը՝ 7 սմ: Բացի տողերի վերջում պակասող մասերից, արձանագրությունը պահպանված է շատ լավ:

Վերականգնելով պակասող մասերը, կարդացվում է այսպես.

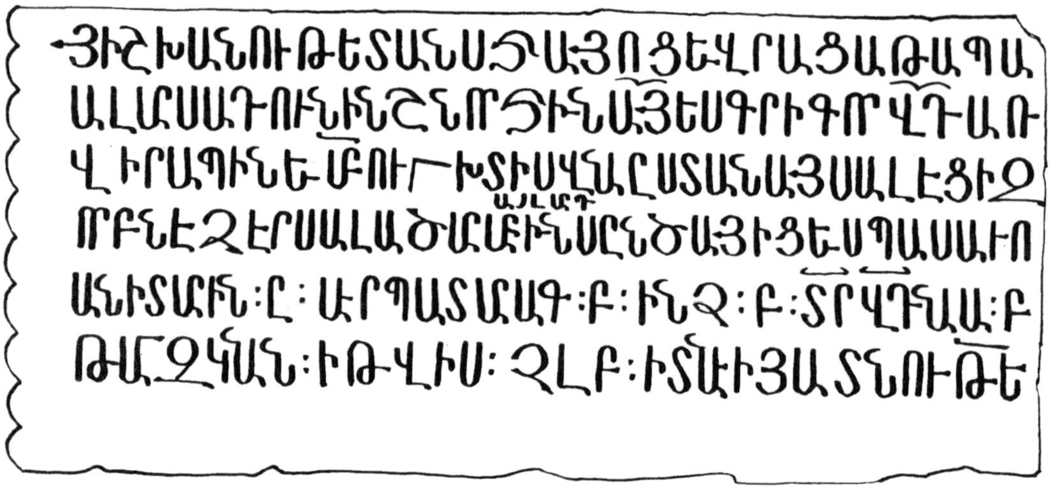

```
ՅԻՇԽԱՆՈՒԹԵՍՏԱՆՁԱՅՈՑԵՎՐԱՑԱԹԱԳԱ
ԱԼԱՍԱԴՈՒՆԻՆՇՆՈՐՀԻՆԱՅԵՍԳՐԻԳՈՐՎԴԱՌ
Վ ԻՐԱՊԻՆԵ ՄՈՒ ԻՏԻՎԿԱՀՍՏԱՆԱՅՍԱԼԵՅԻՁ
ՐԲՆԵՉԵՐՍԱԼԱԾԱՌԻՆՍՆԾԱՅԻՁԵՍՊԱՍԱՐՈ
ԱՆԻՏԱՌԻ։Լ։ԱՐՊԱՏԱԳ։Բ։ԻՆՉ։Բ։ՏՐՎԴԱ։Բ
ԹԱԼՉԿԱՆ։ԻԹ-ՎԻՍ։ՉԼԲ։ԻՏՆԻՅԱՏՆՈՒԹԵ
```

Pl. 4:3

Comments: At the centre of the stone, in the second line of the inscription, a quadrangle sign is visible, which could be the sign of the author of the inscription. In the third line, the letter Վ, in the word ՎԻՐԱՊԻՆ is engraved twice erroneously. In the fourth line it is written ԱՐԱՐԻԻՆՍ, but together with the above letters ԱՅԼ ԱՐԴ, one can read ԱՐԱՐԻ ԱՅԼ ԱՐԴԻԻՆՍ (Kalantar).

11. *The inscription of the owners of the fortress of Keghi*

Written on a massive quadrangle stone (1.62 x 0.67 m), with the right edge similar to the stone of inscription No. 10, with two semi-circular, serrated, broken edges. The stone was found on the south-western slope and removed to the western wall of the church, along with other collected fragments.

The inscription contains seven lines, but it is damaged. The initial (left) portions of the lines are missing, and were probably inscribed on the nearby stone. Besides this, its several initial and final lines are partly damaged and broken. The size of letters is 7 cm.

---

[14] The inscription mentions Vardan the brother of Grigor, the head of the church.

ՅԻՇԽԱՆՈՒԹԵԱՆ ՏԱՆՍ ՀԱՅՈՑ ԵԻ ՎՐԱՑ ԱԹԱՊԱ/⌜Կ ԵԻ ԱՄԻՐՍՊԱՍՆԱԼԱՐ
ՍԱԴՈՒՆԻՆ, ՇՆՈՐՀԻՆ ԱՅ ԵՍ ԳՐԻԳՈՐ Վ(ԱՐ)Դ(ԱՊԵՏ) ԱՌ/⌜ԱՋՆՈՐԴ ⌝
ՎԻՐԱՊԻՆ ԵԻ ՍՈՒՐԲ ՈՒԽՏԻՍ ՎԱՆՔՍՏԱՆԱՅ ՍԱԼԵՑԻ Չ/⌜ԵԿԵՂԵՑԻՍ⌝, ՈՐ
ԲՆԷ ՉԷՐ ՍԱԼԱԾ. ԱՐԱՐԻ ԱՅԼ ԱՐԴԻՒՆՍ ԸՆԾԱՅԻՑ. ԵԻ ՍՊԱՍԱԻՈ/⌜ՐԲ
ԽՈՍՏԱՑԱՆ Ի ՏԱՐԻՆ :Բ: ԱԻՐ ՊԱՏԱՐԱԳ. :Բ: ԻՆՉ, :Բ:
ՏԷՐ Վ(ԱՐ)Դ(Ա)ՆԱ[14], :Բ: ....., :Բ: / ԹԱՄՉԿԱՆՆ. Ի ԹՎԻՍ : ՉԼԲ:
(1283 թվ.) Ի ՏԱՆԻ ՅԱՅՏՆՈՒԹԵԱՆ:

Նկատողություն.

Քարի կենտրոնում, արձանագրության երրորդ տողի վրա փորված է մի նշան, ուղղանկյան գմանությամբ, որ կարող է լինել քարը մշակող վարպետի նշանը: Երրորդ տողում ՎԻՐԱՊԻՆ խոսքի մեջ Վ տառը սխալմամբ փորագրված է երկու անգամ, մեկը կիսամշակ: Չորրորդ տողում գրված է ԱՐԱՐԻԻՆՍ ապա վերևից ավելացրած է ԱՅԼ ԱՐԴ, որով ստացվում է ԱՐԱՐԻ ԱՅԼ ԱՐԴԻԻՆՍ (Աշխ.Ք.):

11. Քեղդ բերդի տերերի (բնակիչների) արձանագրությունը

Գրված է քառանկյունի մասիվ սալաքարի վրա (1,62 x 0,67 մ), որի աջ ծայրը (ըստ արձանագրության ուղղության) No. 10 արձանագրության քարի գմանությամբ վերջանում է զույգ կիսաշրջաններով և ատամնավոր կտրվածքով: Քարն ընկած էր եկեղեցու հարավ-արևմտյան կողմի լանջի վրա. տեղափոխված է ու դրված եկեղեցու արևմտյան պատի մոտ, նույն տեղում հավաքված այլ բեկորների հետ:

Արձանագրությունը յոթ տող է, բայց վնասված է կեսից ավելին: Պակասում է արձանագրության առաջի (ծախ) մասը` տողերի սկիզբը, որ եղել է հարևան քարի վրա` ծախ կողմից: Բացի այդ, նրա սկզբի և վերջի մեկ-երկու տողերը կիսով չափ վնասված են քարի ջարդոտվածության պատճառով: Գրերի երկարությունը` 7 սմ:

---

[14] Վանքի առաջնորդ Գրիգոր վարդապետի եղբայրը:

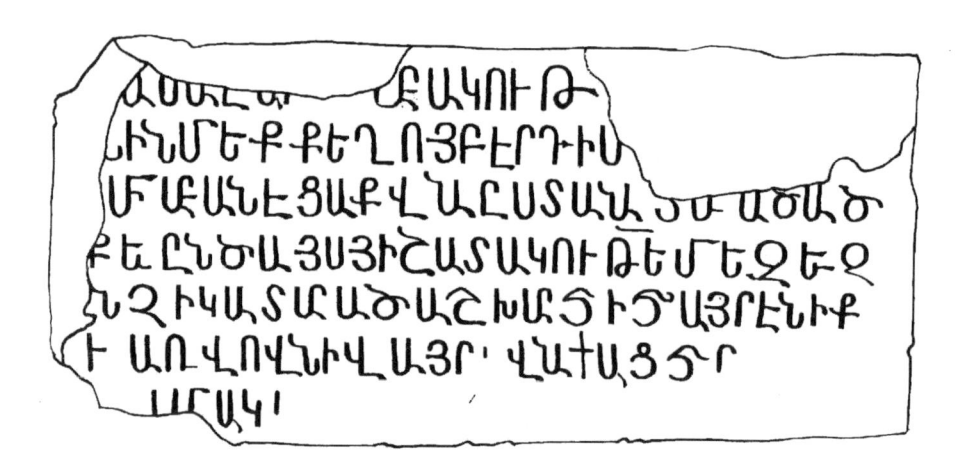

Comment: The first line of the inscription can be recovered as follows (H.M., G.S.):

ԱՄԻՐՊԱՍԱԼԱՐ ԱԹԱԲԱԿՈՒԹԵԱՆ ՍԱԴՈՒՆԻ... (Հ.Մ., Գ.Ս.):

12. Inscription about a water-channel (1323)

The inscription is written on a stone that was found on the eastern slope, above the road. It was also removed to the western wall of the church. The stone is quadrangle, and its surface is completely covered with an inscription of five lines. It differs from the other inscriptions of Vanstan in its large number of abbreviations and the size of its letters. The last two or three letters of each line, as well as the last line (containing the date), are damaged.

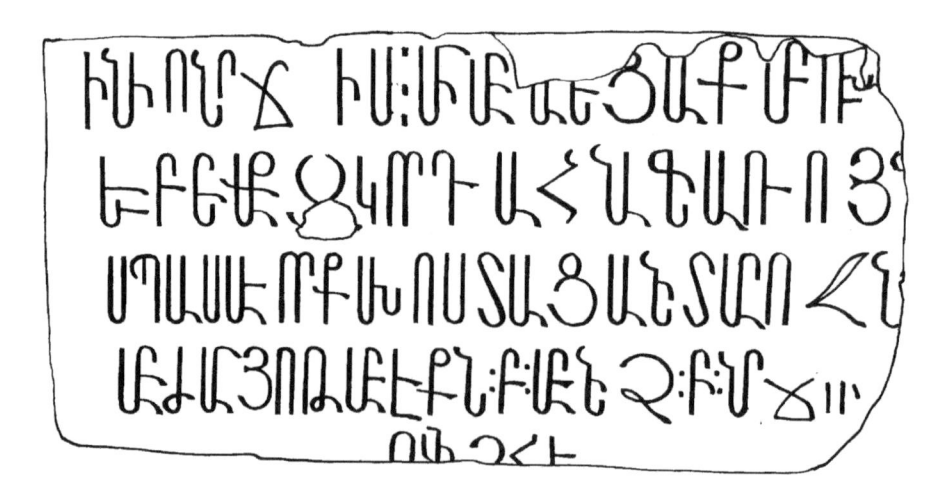

Pl. 5:2

---

[15] Keghi berd mentioned in the inscription is a mediaeval fortress located 4 km west of Vanstan. It was one of the main fortresses of the Bagratuni princes, later passed on to the Zakarian princes.

[16] ԿՈՐԴԱՀԱՆ means a non-cultivated site (H. Ajarjan, *op. cit.* 2, p. 646).

..... ⌜ՍՊ⌝ԱՍԱԼԱՐ .....ԱԿՈՒԹ.....

..... ⌜Ն⌝ԻՆ ՄԵՔ ՔԵՂՈՑ ԲԵՐԴԻՍ[15] .....

..... ՄԻԱԲԱՆԵՑԱՔ ՎԱՆՔՍՏԱՆԱՅ ՍՈՒՐԲ ԱԾԱԾ/

..... Ք ԵՒ ԸՆԾԱՅՍ ՅԻՇԱՏԱԿՈՒԹ⌜ԵԱՆ⌝ ՄԵՋ ԵՒ/

Չ⌜ԱՒԱԿԱՑ ՄԵՐՈՑ ՄԻ⌝Ն2 Ի ԿԱՏԱՐԱԾ ԱՇԽԱՐՀԻ ՀԱՅՐԵՆԻՔ/

..... ⌜Ո⌝Ի ԱՌՎՈՎՆ Ի ՎԱՅՐ ՎԱՆԱՑ ՀՐ /

..... ԿՍԱԿԱ ..... Հ .....:

Նկատողություն

Արձանագրության առաջին տողում վերծանվում է.

... ⌜ԱՄԻՐՍՊ⌝⌜ԱՄ⌝ԱԼԱՐ ԱԹ⌜ԱԲԱԿՈՒԹ⌝ԵԱՆ ՍԱԴՈՒՆԻ⌝... (Հ.Մ., Գ.Ս.):

12. *Արձանագրություն առու բերելու մասին (1323 թվ.)*

Այս արձանագրությունը գրված է մի քարի վրա, որ գտնվեց եկեղեցու արևելյան կողմի գառիվայրին՝ ճանապարհի գլխին ու փոխադրված է եկեղեցու արևմտյան պատի մոտ, այլ հուշարձանների հավաքման տեղը:

Քարը քառանկյունի է, մի երեսն ամբողջովին ծածկված է հինգ տող արձանագրությամբ: Այն տարբերվում է Վանստանի մյուս արձանագրություններից իր ծվատների ավելի մեծ քանակությամբ և գրերի երկարությամբ: Տողերի վերջին երկու-երեք գրերը, ինչպես նաև վերջին տողը, որ թվականն է՝ վնասված են:

..... ՆԱՐԵԻՍՍ (?) ՄԻԱԲԱՆԵՑԱՔ ՍՈՒՐԲ ՈՒԽ⌜ՏԻՍ⌝ / ԵՒ ԲԵՐԱՔ

ՁԿՈՐԴԱՀԱՆԻՆ[16] ԱՌՈՅ⌜Ն ԵՒ⌝ / ՍՊԱՍԱԽՈՐՔՍ ԽՈՍՏԱՅԱՆ Ի ՏԱՐՈՋ⌜Ն⌝

:Դ:⌝/ ԱԻՐ ԺԱՄ ՅՈՒԹԱԻՐԵՔՆ. :Բ: ԱԻՐ ԻՆՁ, :Բ:

ՆԱՐԵՍԻ (?)/⌜ԹՎԻՆ ՁՀԷ⌝ (1328 թվ):

---

[15] Միջնադարյան ամրոց, գտնվում է Վանստանից մոտ 4 կմ արևելք, եղել է Բագրատունյաց հզոր ամրոցներից մեկը, հետագայում անցել է Զաքարյան իշխաններին: Բազմիցս հիշատակվում է մատենագրական աղբյուրներում:

[16] «Խոպան, անմշակ հող» (Հ.Աճառյան, Հայերեն արմատական բառարան, հտ. 2, Երևան, 1973, էջ 646):

Comments: At least one line from the beginning of the inscription is missing; it contained the name of Nrjis' husband, the benefactor of the church. At the end of the first line one can read ԻՆ ԻՄ of which ԻՆ is the end of the word ԱՄՈՒՍԻՆ written in the previous line; after it one can read the name ՆՐՃԻՍ. The same in the fourth line. (H.M., G.S.)

13. *Tomb inscription*

To the west of the church — where the necropolis is located — a grave-stone (1.52 x 0.54 m) was found *in situ*. On its surface: two semicircles and a human head-like curve; below, an inscription of 6 lines:

Comments: The letter in the date can be read as Ձ, which yields 1340 (Kalantar).

There are three inscriptions on the surviving (lower) part of the western wall, on its northern edge. The first two are remarkable among the Vanstan inscriptions in that they have a large number of abbreviations (often rather complicated).

```
ԱՅԼԷ
ՀԱԿԱՐ
ԱՀԱԽԵ
ՐԴՈՅ
ՍԱՐԿԵ
ՉՁԹ։
```

Pl. 5:3

14. *Inscription of Avrtakh Hovhannes*

This text is inscribed on an elongated stone, in the top row, with semicircular eaves. The inscription contains two long lines, the first of which is in rather bad condition. All the letters along this line are partly damaged due to the break of the stone. Besides this, the line presumably continued on the adjacent stone, which is missing. This stone also has a central quadrangle sign (as in No. 10), which again is presumably the author's sign, since it was engraved in the stone before the inscription.

Restoring the abbreviations and the missing and damaged parts, we read:

Նկատողություն

Արձանագրության սկզբից պակասում է առնվազն մեկ տող, որտեղ եղել է նվիրատուի՝ Նրճիսի ամուսնու անունը: Պահպանված առաջին տողի սկզբում վերծանվում է ԻՆ ԻՄ: ԻՆ-ը նախորդ տողում փորագրված ԱՄՈՒՍԻՆ բառի վերջավորությունն է, որից հետո կնոջ անունը վերծանվում է ՆՐՃԻՍ: Նույնը և չորրորդ տողում (Հ.Մ., Գ.Ս.):

13. *Դամբարանային արձանագրություն*

Եկեղեցու արևմտյան հրապարակում, ուր հանգստարանն է, իր նախկին տեղում պահպանվել է մի շիրմաքար (1,52 x 0,54 մ): Երեսի կողմից ունի զույգ կիսաշրջան զարդերիգ և վերին ծայրում մարդու գլխի գծանկար, որի տակ արձանագրությունն է 6 կարճ տողերով.

ԱՅՍ Է / ՀԱՆԿԻՍՏ / ՍՀԱԹԻՆ, / ՈՐԴՈՑ / ՍԱՐԳՍԻՆ. / ՉԺԹ

(1270 թվ.):

Նկատողություն

Թվականի մեջ գիրը կարող է կարդացվել և Ձ (ուրեմն՝ 1340թ.) (Ա₂խ.Ք.):

Արևմտյան պատի պահպանված (ներքևի) մասի վրա, նրա հյուսիսային ծայրին մոտ, գրված է երեք արձանագրություն: Սրանցից առաջին երկուսը իրենց ծովպատների շատությամբ և կրճատումներով, հնչյուն բավականին բարդ ձևի, առանձնանում են Վանստանի արձանագրությունների մեջ:

14. *Ալրքախ Հովհաննեսի արձանագրությունը*

Գրված է ամենավերևի շարքի մի երկարավուն քարի վրա, որն իր վերևի եզերքում կիսաշրջանով և ակոսով հարդարված քիվ ունի: Արձանագրությունը երկու երկար տողից է, որից վերին տողը շատ վատ է պահպանվել: Նրա գրերը տողի ամբողջ երկարությամբ, կիսով չափ ոչնչացել են քարի եզերքի ջարդվածության պատճառով:

Անկախ դրանից, այդ տողն ըստ երևույթին, շարունակվելիս է եղել նաև հարևան քարի վրա, որն այժմ չկա: Այս արձանագրության քարը ևս իր կենտրոնական մասում ունի ուղղանկյան ճեղք, նման No.10-ին, որն ինչպես ասացի, հավանաբար քարը մշակող վարպետի նշանն է, քանի որ այն եղել է քարի վրա՝ արձանագրելուց առաջ:

Լրացնելով կրճատումները, բանալով ծովպատները և վերականգնելով փչացած, ոչնչացած մասերը, արձանագրությունը կարդացվում է այսպես.

25

[Inscription image, Pl. 6:1]

Pl. 6:1

Comments: ԱԽԹԱԽ in the first line is the title of the benefactor and is an unknown word.[18] Because the upper part of the inscription is missing, and because it can be an abbreviated form, it can be read also as ԱԻՐԹԱԽ. There is a letter Պ at the end of the first line, presumably the gift was a cheese (Kalantar).

15. *Tukhtung's inscription*

In the second row of the surviving part of the western wall of the church, on two stones, below the previous inscription, another two-line inscription is engraved, quite similar to the previous one. The inscription is in quite good condition, and therefore the broken parts can be easily recovered.

Restoring the damaged parts and expanding the abbreviations, we read as shown on p. 27.

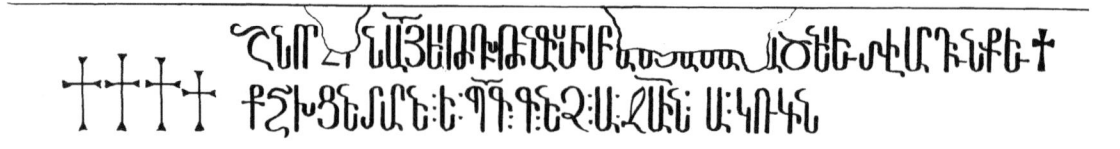

[Inscription image, Pl. 6:1 lower]

Pl. 6:1 (lower inscription)

---

[17] The church mentioned in the inscription concerns Khor Virap, the religious centre of Ararat state.

[18] This word has been the focus of a special study by S. Avagian. He compared it with the Mongolian word 'ortak' or 'urtak' which he translated as 'friend', 'colleague' (S. Avagian, *Analysis of Stone-Inscriptions*, Erevan, 1978, p. 340-342).

ԿԱՍԱԽՆ ԱՅ ԵՍ ԱԻԹԱԽ (?) (ԱԻՐԹԱԽ ?) ՅՈՎԱՆԵՍ ՄԻԱԲԱՆԵՑԱ

ՍՈՒՐԲ ՎԱՆԻՍ[17] ԵՒ ՎԱՆՔՍՏԱՆԻ ՍՈՒՐԲ ԱԾԱԾՆԻՆ ԵՒ ԵՏՈՒ ԱՐԴԻՒՆՍ

:Կ: ԼԻՏՐ Պ/ .... ⌈ԵՒ ՍՊԱՍԱԽՈՐՔՍ⌉ ԵՏՈՒՆ Ի ՏԱՐՈՋՆ :Բ:

ԱԻՐ ՊԱՏԱՐԱԳԵԼ ՁՔՐԻՍՏՈՍ Ի ՏԱՆԻ ՅՈՎԱՆՈՒ :Ա: ԻՆՉ ԵՒ :Ա:

ԻՄ ՄԱԻՐՆ ՍԻՐԱՍԱՐԳԻՆ:

Նկատողություն

Առաջին տողում **ԱԻԹԱԽ** (?) խոսքը, որ նվիրատուի կոչումն է, անձանոթ բառ է[18], քանի որ գրերի վերին մասերը չկան, որոշ չէ նրա ընթերցումը, կարող էր նա ծոպատված լինել և այդ դեպքում կարդացվել **ԱԻՐԹԱԽ**, կամ մի այլ կերպ։ Առաջին տողի վերջում պահպանվել է միայն բառի սկզբնատառը՝ **Պ**. գուցե նվերը եղել է պանիր (Աշխ.Ք.):

15. Թուխբունչի արձանագրությունը

Եկեղեցու արևմտյան պատի պահպանված մասի. երկրորդ շարքում (վերևից), որ քիչ ավելի դուրս է ընկած քան առաջինը, հիմնաշարի հեևց վերևում, երկու քարի վրա, նախորդ արձանագրության տակ, գտնվում է երկրորդ արձանագրությունը, նույնպես երկու տողից և գրված է միակերպ՝ առաջինի նման, նրա բոլոր առանձնահատկություններով։ Արձանագրությունը բավականաչափ լավ է պահպանված, քարի ջարդված մասերում վնասված բառերը հեշտությամբ վերականգնվում են։

Լրացնելով կրճատումները, բացալով ծոպատները և վերականգնելով վնասված, ոչնչացած մասերը, արձանագրությունը կարդացվում է այսպես.

ՇՆՈՐՀԻՒՆ ԱՅ ԵՍ ԹՈՒԽԹՈՒՆԳՍ ՄԻԱԲԱՆԵՑԱ ՍՈՒՐԲ ԱԾԱԾՆԻՍ

ԵՒ ՏՎԻ ԱՐԴԻՒՆՔ ԵՒ / Ք(Ա)Հ(ԱՆԱՅՔ) Խ(ՈՍՏԱ)Յ(ԱՆ) Ի ՏԱՐԻՆ

:Ե: Պ(ԱՏԱՐԱ)Գ :Գ: ԻՆՉ, :Ա: ՁԱԼԱԼԻՆ, :Ա: ԿՈՒԿԻՆ:

---

[17] Նվիրատուն այստեղ նկատի ունի Հայոց Եկեղեցու Արարատյան թեմական կենտրոն Խոր Վիրապի վանքը:

[18] Այս տերմինը հատուկ ուսումնասիրության է ենթարկել հայտնի վիմագրագետ Ս.Ավագյանը: Վերջինս այն համեմատելով մոնղոլական ortak և urtak տերմինների հետ, գտնում է, որ այն պետք է ստուգաբանել ույղուրերեն «ընկեր, ընկերակից, պաշտոնակից» (Ս.Ավագյան, Վիմական արձանագրությունների բառքննություն, Երևան, 1978, էջ 340-342):

16. Simon's inscription

On the same wall, on the continuation of inscription No. 15, the third inscription is located – a short line of small fussy letters. I present this inscription, which is evidently of a later period, for the sake of completeness of the inscriptions of the western wall:

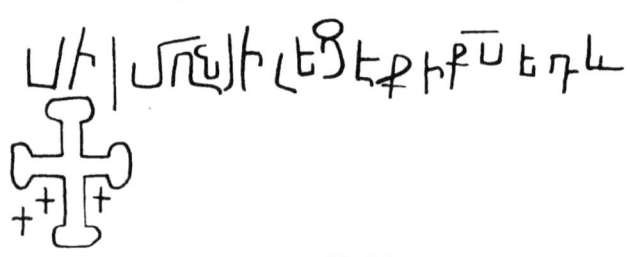

Սի | մոնի լեցէքիքս եդև

Pl. 6:1

17. Fragment of an inscription found inside the church

From the same place as other inscriptions inside the church. The surviving letters form three lines, and presumably are the top parts of an inscription:

Թ

ՇՆ

ՄՍ

18. Fragment of a large-letter inscription, again found inside the church

ՏՈՒՐՄ

19. Inscription of Mkhitar and Mkhitarich

The inscription was found on the pedestal of a cross-stone, removed from its place long ago, and is now located in the village, near the entrance of a house, where it serves as a water reservoir. The inscription contains three lines written clearly on the surface of the pedestal, without any breaks:

ԹՎՍԾ ԲԱԵԻԱՍՈՒՄԲՄԱԾԱՆԻՍ
ՈՂՈՐՄԵԱՋԲԱԵՋԲԱՀԻՆԵ
ԾՆՈՂԱՑՆՈՑԱՎԼ

Pl. 6:2

16. *Սիմոնի արձանագրությունը*

Մինույն առնմտյան պատի վրա, No. 15 արձանագրության վերջին տողի շարունակության վրա գտնվում է երրորդ արձանագրությունը, որը մի կարճ տողով գրված է հասարակ խզվածքով և մանրագրերով։ Այս արձանագրությունը, որ անտարակույս ուշ ժամանակի գործ է, մեջ եմ բերում այստեղ նրա համար, որպեսզի լրիվ լինի առնմտյան պատի արձանագրությունների թիվը, չհետևելով ժամանակագրական կարգին։

ՍԻՄՈՆ ՅԻՇԵՑԷՔ Ի Ք̄Ս ԵՂԵԻ։

17. *Արձանագրության հատված, խոշոր գրերով, գտնված է եկեղեցում* և դրված նույն տեղում, մյուս արձանագրությունների մեջ։ Պահպանված գրերը երեք տարբեր տողերից են, հավանաբար արձանագրության սկզբի մասից։

Թ⌈Վ⌉.....

ՇՆ⌈ՈՐՀԻՆ ԱՅ⌉.....

ՄՍ.....։

18. *Արձանագրության հատված, խոշոր գրերով, նույնպես գտնված եկեղեցու ավերակների վրա.*

.....ՏՈՒՐ Մ⌈ԵՁ⌉....

19. *Մխիթարի և Մխիթարիչի արձանագրությունը*

Արձանագրությունը գտնվում է մի խաչքարի պատվանդանի վրա, որը վաղուց ընկած է իր տեղից։ Ներկայումս գյուղի մեջ, մի տան դռան առաջ դրված է իբրև ավազան՝ աղբյուրի ջրի տակ։ Արձանագրությունը երեք տող է, պատվանդանի երեսի վրա, գրված է պարզ և վնասված տեղեր չունի։

Ք⌊ՐԻՍՏՈ⌋Ս⌊ԱՍՏՈՒԱ⌋Ծ ԲԱՐԵԽԱՒՍՈՒԹ⌊ԵԱՄԲ ՍՈՒՐԲ ԱԾԱԾՆԻՍ, /
ՈՂՈՐՄԵԱ ՄԽԻԹԱՐԱ ԵՒ ՄԽԻԹԱՐԻՉԻՆ ԵՒ / ԾՆՈՂԱՑ ՆՈՑԱ, ԱՄ⌊ԵՅՆ։

20. Inscription of Mkhitarich

On the eastern slope, near the road, a quadrangle stone (0.97 x 0.74 m) was excavated, with three crosses (the middle one bigger than the others) under an engraved arch. The inscription above the arch contains 7 lines, the size of letters is 7 cm.

ՄԵՂ ՈԱՅՍՄՆԻԹ
ԻՇԵՏՈՒՋՉՈՂՈՅԱՅԳԻՆՑԵ
ՐԻՑՐՆԻՄՐՈՒԽ ՍԵԱՈՒ․ՄԷԱՑ
ԺՄԻՆՉ ՉՎԱԴԱՎԱ
ՈՒԵՐ ՈՎԽԱՓ
ՆԷԴԱՏ
ԻՅԱՅ

21. Fragment of an inscription

Upper part of a cross-stone, along with a wicked ornament; remnants of a red color. One word has survived:

ՄԽԻԹԱ

Comments: This stone has also been removed from a wall of a house in Imirzek and is now placed together with other inscription-stones (Kalantar).

22. Gishuk's inscription

On the eastern slope, precisely to the south-east of the church, above the apricot tree, a stone was excavated with a five-line inscription. The lower edge of the stone is broken, and therefore the last line is incomplete. Nevertheless, by its content the inscription can be considered to be complete. The size of the letters is 8 cm.

ԿԱՄՆԱՅԵՍԳԻՇՈՒԿՍ
ԵԱՍԻԿԱՏՈՒՂ․Խ․ԴԱՅ․
ԻՄՈՒԽՏԱՏՐԳՈՐԳԵԱՅԼԵ
ՂԲԱՓՍՏՈՒՆԼԵՉ․Բ․ԱՐ
ԺԱՄՏԱՆԻ ՄԽԱՉ․

20. *Մխիթարիչի արձանագրությունը*

Եկեղեցու արևելյան լանջին, ճանապարհի տակ, պեղված է մի քառանկյունի քար՝ խաչերով (0,97 x 0,74 մ), որի երեսի ներքին կեսում, սլաքավոր կամարի տակ փորված են երեք խաչեր, մի շարքի, միջինը մի քիչ ավելի մեծ: Կամարի վերևում տեղավորված է արձանագրությունը՝ 7 տող, գրերի երկարությունը՝ 7 սմ:

ՍԵՂ⸢ԱՊԱՐՏ ԾԱ⸣ԴԱՅՍ ՄԽԻԹ⸢ԱՐ/ԻՉ

ԵՏՈՒ ՉՉՈՂՈՒՅ ԱՅԳԻՆ ՅԵՐ/ԻՉ ՄԻՆ

Ի ՍՈՒՐԲ ՈՒԽ⸢ՏՍ⸣ ԵԻ ԱՌԻ :Ա: ԱԻՐ/

ԺԱՄ ԻՆՉ ՉՎԱՐԴԱՎԱ/Ռ

ԱԻՐ: ՈՎ ԽԱՓ/ԱՆԷ ԴԱՏ/Ի

ՅԱՍՏՈՒԾՈյ3:

21. *Արձանագրության հատված խաչքարի շրջանակի վերին մասում*, որն ունի հյուսվածքային քանդակ, անգամ կարմիր ներկի հետքեր. պահպանվել է մեկ բառ.

ՄԽԻԹԱ⸢Ր⸣

Նկատողություն

Այս բեկորը նույնպես հանված է Իմիրզեկցոց նոր շենքերի պատերից և դրված մյուս արձանագրությունների հետ եկեղեցու տեղում (Ա₂խ.Ք.):

22. *Գիշուկի արձանագրությունը*

Արևելյան լանջի վրա, եկեղեցու ճիշտ հարավարևելյան անկյան ուղղությամբ, ճանապարհից ցած, ծիրանի ծառի անմիջապես վերևում պեղված է մի քար, որ ունի հինգ տող արձանագրություն: Քարի ներքին եզերքը կոտրված է, և արձանագրության վերջին տողը թերի է: Ըստ բովանդակության արձանագրությունը կարելի է ավարտված համարել: Գրերի երկարությունը՝ 8 սմ.

ԿԱՄԱՒՆ Ա̄Յ ԵՍ ԳԻՇՈՒԿԱՍ / ԵԻ

ՄԻՍԻԿԱՍ ՏՈՒԱՔ :Խ: ԴԱՀ(ԵԿԱՆ) /

Ի ՍՈՒՐԲ ՈՒԽՏԻՍ. ՏԵՐ ԳՈՐԳ ԵԻ ԱՅԼ

Ե/ՂԲԱՐՔՍ ՏՈՒԻՆ ՄԵՉ :Բ: ԱԻՐ /

ԺԱՄ Ի ՏԱՆԻ ՍՈՒՐԲ ԽԱ⸢ՉԻՆ⸣:

23. *Fragment of an inscription*

A stone (1.10 x 0.49 m) extracted from a coarse wall in the area of the southern altar carries the last two lines of an incomplete inscription. In the size and style of the letters this inscription corresponds to No. 22. Both stones were found inside the church, in front of the table.

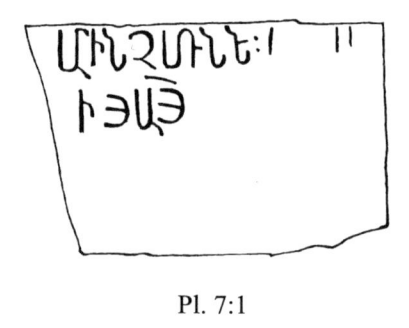

Pl. 7:1

24. *Fragment of an inscription*

Found near the water channel, below the slope, this stone exhibits an engraved cross with a pair of circles on its edges. Around the cross, along the whole surface of the stone, there is an incomplete six-line inscription. It presumably continued below the cross, on a part which is missing. The size of the letters is 8 cm.

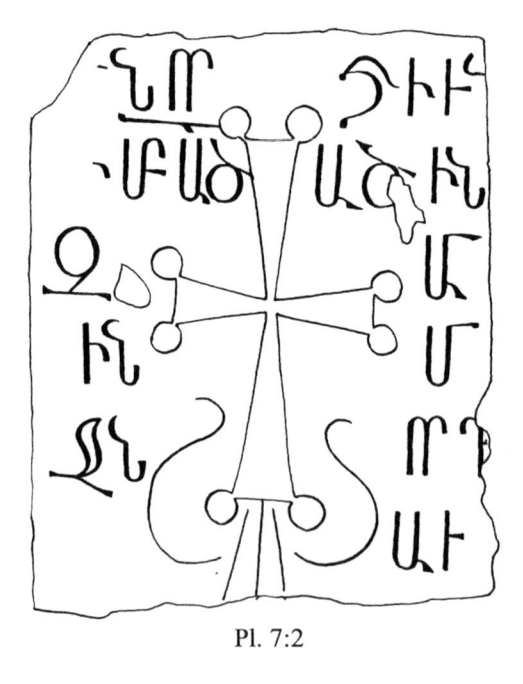

Pl. 7:2

On the eastern slope, near the north-east corner of the church, an excavated stone (1.35 x 0.60m) revealed inscriptions on one side, one under the other. The lower inscription has bigger letters than the upper one.

23. *Արձանագրության հատված*

Եկեղեցու հարավային խորանի տեղում շինած հարդանոցի չոր շարված պատից հանվել է մի քար (1,10 x 0,49 մ), որի վրա կա քերի արձանագրության վերջին երկու տողերը։ Արձանագրությունն իր տողերի երկարությամբ և գրերի տեսակով կարող է համապատասխանել № 22 արձանագրությանը։ Երկու քարն էլ դրված են եկեղեցու մեջ, սեղանի առաջ։

⌈:Ա: ԺԿՄ ԻՆՉ ԱՌՆԵՆ,

⌈:Ա:⌉ ՀՈՌ⌈ՈՍԻՍՄ (?). ՈՎ

ԽԱՓԱՆԻ ԴԱՏ⌈Ի ՅԱՍՏՈՒԾՈ:

24. *Արձանագրության հատված*

Եկեղեցուց հարավ-արևելք, լանջի տակ, առվակի մոտ կողքի վրա ընկած է մի քար, վրան փորված խաչով, որի ծայրերը վերջանում են զույգ գնդիկներով։ Խաչի շուրջը, քարի ամբողջ երեսով մեկ, բռնում է արձանագրությունը՝ վեց տողի վրա։ Արձանագրությունը չի վերջանում, նրա շարունակությունը, հավանաբար, եղել է խաչի ներքևում, որը չի պահպանվել։ Գրերի երկարությունը՝ 8 սմ։

⌈ՇՆՈՐՀԻ⌈Ն⌉/

ՍՈՒՐԲ ԱԾԱԾԻՆ /

ՁԱՄ / ԻՆ

Մ / (Ի)ՁՆՈՐԴԱԻ......

Արևելյան լանջի վրա, եկեղեցու հարավ-արևելյան անկյան ուղղությամբ, ճանապարհի գլխին պեղված մի քար (1,35 x 0,60 մ), իր երեսի կողմի վրա ունի արձանագրություն՝ գրված մեկը մյուսի տակ։ Ներքևի արձանագրությունը համեմատաբար ավելի խոշորագիր է, քան վերևինը։

25. Inscription of Sargis Gergantz

This inscription was found on a stone (1.35 x 0.60 m) excavated on the south-eastern slope, above the road. The inscription contains two lines, which presumably continued on the neighbouring stone. In addition, the first line is half-damaged because of the broken edges of the stone. The size of the letters is 5.5 cm.

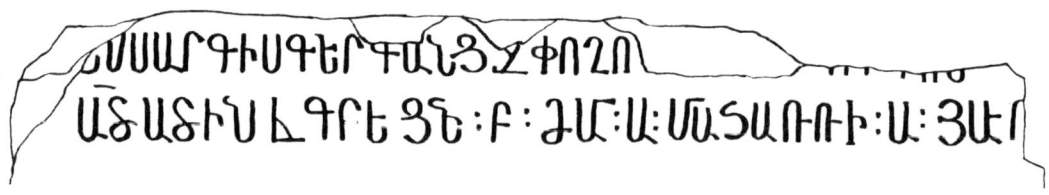

Pl. 7:3

26. The inscription of Patutik and Mamikhatun

The text has three complete lines. The size of the letters is 8.5 cm. On the steep southern slope, close to the canyon and under the tall poplars, were gathered several sculptured stones from the church, two of them with inscriptions. Both of these stones are of similar shape, and inscribed in a similar way. Presumably they are parts of the same inscription.

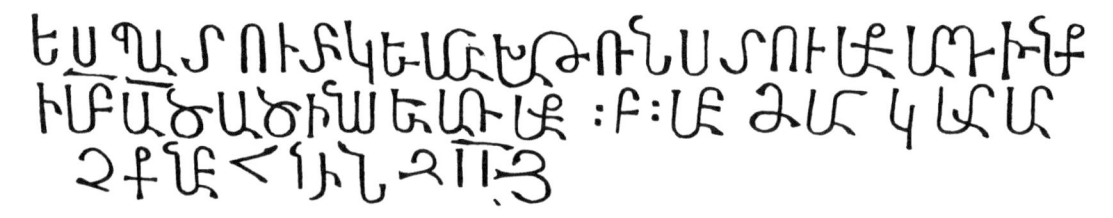

Pl. 7:3

27. Fragment of an inscription

On one of these stones (with a cavity and intertwined carvings) are four damaged lines. The size of the letters is 6.5 cm.

Pl. 8:1

25. *Սարգիս Գերգանցի արձանագրությունը*

Վերևի արձանագրությունը երկու տողից է, որը չի վերջանում այս քարի վրա և, հավանաբար, շարունակվելիս է եղել հարևան քարին: Բացի այդ առաջին տողը կիսով չափ փչացած է քարի եզերքների ջարդվածության պատճառով. գրերի երկարությունը՝ 5,5 սմ.

ԵՍ ՍԱՐԳԻՍ ԳԵՐԳԱՆՑ ԶՓՈՂՈ..... ⌈ՍՈՒՐԲ⌉/ ԱԾԱԾԻՆՍ ԵՒ ԳՐԵՑԻՆ

:Բ: ԺԱՄ, :Ա: ՍԱՀԱՌՈՒ, :Ա: ՅԱԽՈՒՐՆ......:

26. *Պատուտիկի և Մամիխաթունի արձանագրությունը*

Ներքևի արձանագրությունը երեք տողից է, լրիվ և լավ պահպանված. գրերի երկարությունը՝ 8,5 սմ.

ԵՍ ՊԱՏՈՒՏԻԿ ԵՒ ՄԱՄԻԽԱԹՈՒՆՍ ՏՈՒԱՔ ԱՐԴԻՆՔ / Ի ՍՈՒՐԲ

ԱԾԱԾԻՆՍ ԵՒ ԱՌԱՔ :Բ: ԱԻՐ ԺԱՄ. ԿԱՏԱՐ/ԻՉՔՆ ԱԻՐՀՆԻՆ ՅԱՍՏՈՒԾՈՅ:

Արնեկյան թեք լանջի վրա, եկեղեցուց ուղիղ հյուսիս-արևելք, լանջի մոտ, միջին մասում (քիչ ավելի մոտ ձորին), բարձր բարդիների տակ, հավաքված են եկեղեցու մի քանի քանդակազարդ քարեր, որոնցից երկուսն ունեն արձանագրություն:

Երկու քարն էլ խորշի պսակի մասեր են, որոնց կողերն արձանագրված են միաշավի ձևով և հնագրական միանման առանձնահատկություններով: Հավանաբար երկուսն էլ մի արձանագրության մասեր են:

27. *Արձանագրության հատված*

Այս քարերից մեկը, որ խորշի վերին ծայրից է՝ խոռոչի մասով և հյուսվածքային քանդակով, կողքի վրա ունի վնասված արձանագրություն չորս տողից, գրերի երկարությունը՝ 6,5 սմ.

...ՍԱՅԱՊԷ .../... ՋՎԱՅԻ Ո.../

...ԵՏ :Ծ: ԴԱՀ (ԵԿԱՆ).../

...ՆՍԱ :Ա: ԱԻՐ...:

28. *Fragment of an inscription*

The fragment has a fraction of a cavity and the remnants of a pair of false arches. On one side it exhibits an inscription of five lines, the first line being totally damaged. The size of the letters is 6.5 cm.

Ա...ԴԷ
ՐԵԱՅ:
ԽՄՔՐ
ԻՐՆ.ԵԻ

Pl. 8:1

29. *Fragment of an inscription*

On a quadrangle stone (0.95 x 0.72 m) excavated on the steep eastern slope, below the road. The stone has an engraved cross under an arch. Upon the arch there is a very damaged four-line inscription. The size of the letters is 7.5 cm.

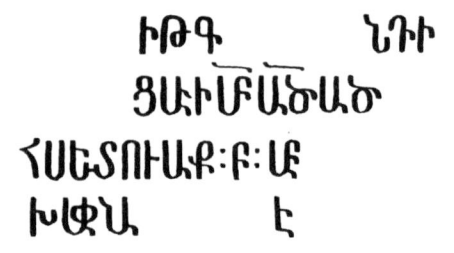

ԻԹԳ   ՆԴԻ
ՅԱԻՄԱԾԱԾ
ՀԱԵՏՈՒԱՔ:Բ:ԱՔ
ԽՓՆ   Է

30. *Fragment of an inscription*

Below the canyon of willows (down to the east from the church), close to the road, in a simple wall in the bushes along the bank of the river Azat, we found a small, broken cross-stone (khachkar) which had apparently rolled down there from above. The sides of the khachkar have the following inscription:

ԿԱԿՆԵՑ

Ե   ԾՆՈՂԱ

28. Արձանագրության հատված

Խորշի քար, ունի վրան խորոչի մաս և զույգ կիսասյուների (կեղծ կամարների) մնացորդներ: Մի կողքի վրա ունի արձանագրության մնացորդ՝ հինգ տող որոնցից առաջին տողը բոլորովին ոչնչացած է, գրերի երկարությունը՝ 6,5 սմ.

...ԱՆՈՒԹԵԱՆ /... ՈՐԵԱՑ

:Ծ: .../.... ԵԻ ՄԵՔ

ՏՈՒԱՔ /....ԱԻՐՆ, ԵԻ ...:

Հիշյալ քարերը ընդհանուր առմամբ պահպանել են 9 տողի մասեր մի անհայտ մեծ արձանագրությունից:

29. Արձանագրության հատված

Արևելյան թեք լանջի վրա, եկեղեցու հարավ-արևելյան անկյան ուղղությամբ, ճանապարհի ներքևում բացվեց մի քառանկյունի սալանման քար (0,95 x 0,72 մ), որն ունի սլաքավոր ռելեֆ խաչի նշան, գետեղված կամարի տակ: Կամարի վերևում գտնվում է սաստիկ վնասված մի արձանագրություն՝ 4 տողից, գրերի երկարությունը՝ 7,5 սմ.

...Ի ԹԳ ....ՆԴԻ .../⌈ՄԻԱԲԱՆԵ⌉ՅԱԻ Ի

ՍՈՒՐԲ ԱԾԱԾ⌈ԻՆՍ.../....ՀՍ, ԵԻ ՏՈՒԱՔ

:Բ: ԱԻՐ ⌈ԺԱՄ Ի ՏԱԻՆԻ ... ՈՎ⌉/

ԽԱՓԱՆԷ...:

30. Արձանագրության հատված

«Ուռիների ձորի» (իջնում է եկեղեցու արևելյան կողմով) ներքևում, ճանապարհի մոտ, Ազատ գետի ափին, մասուրների խիտ թփերով ծածկված մի հասարակ պատաշարի մեջ գտնվեց ոչ մեծ, կոտրված մի խաչքար, որն ըստ երևույթին վերևից գլորվելով թեք լանջի վրայով հասել է այդտեղ: Այդ խաչքարի շրջանակի կողերի վրա կարդացվում է.

...ԿԱՆԿՆԵՑ.../

Ե...ԾՆՈՂԱՅՆ...:

31. *Benefaction inscription*

Among the stones extracted from the walls of the houses of Imirzek we found one (1.40 x 0.67 m) having a four-line inscription with large letters. The area below the inscription is filled by crosses. One edge of the stone is broken, therefore the first 4-6 letters in each line are missing. Restoring these parts as much as possible, we read as shown on p. 39.

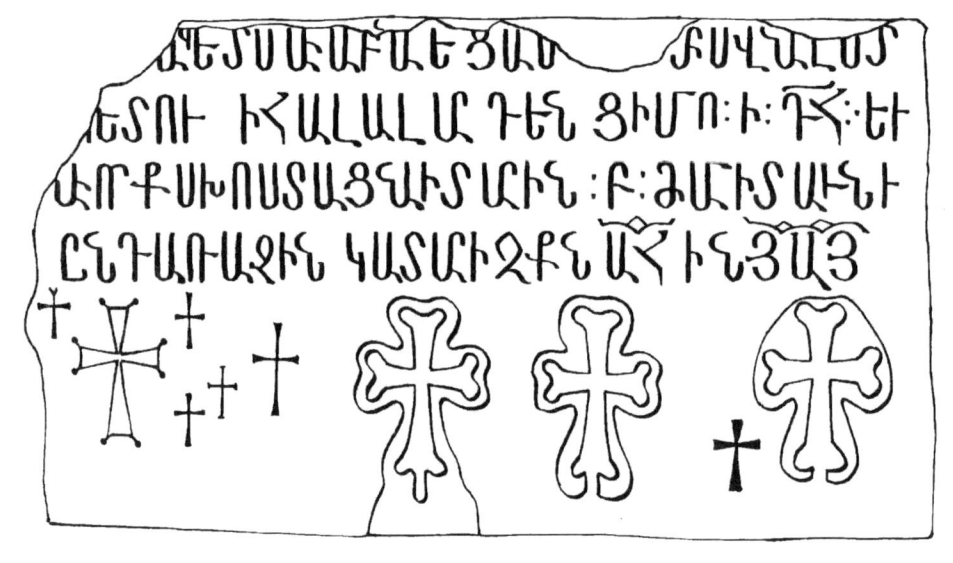

Pl. 8:2

Comments: In the first line only the last part of the name of the benefactor has survived: ԱՂԵՏՍ or ԱՊԵՏՍ, perhaps yielding Hayrapet or Nahapet. (Kalantar)

32. *The inscription of bishop Khad*

Below the southern rock, above the road, there are several stones, smoothed for use in the nearby threshing floor. A roughly processed grave-stone (1.99 x 0.51 m) with broken edges was found among them. It has a simply engraved, quadrangle frame; it bears the drawing of a bishop's crown, and below it, along the whole length of the stone, that of a bishop's sceptre, with a three line inscription on both sides:

ԱԵՀԱ

ԿԵՏ

ԽԵՊ

---

[19] Bishop Khad is mentioned as the scribe of one of the manuscripts recopied in Vanstan in 1560 (G. Hovsepian, *Khaghbakiank or Proshiank in Armenian History* 3, New York, 1942-43, p. 125).

31. Նվիրատվական արձանագրության

Իմիրզեկցոց հասարակ շենքերի պատերից հանված բեկորների մեջ կա նաև մի քար (1,40 x 0,67 մ), որ ունի իր ամբողջ երկարությամբ գրված չորս տող խոշորատառ արձանագրություն: Արձանագրության տակ մնացած ազատ տարածությունը լրացրած է խաչանշաններով: Քարի մի ծայրը կոտրված է, ուստի և ոչնչացել են արձանագրության տողերի սկիզբը՝ 4-6 գիր յուրաքանչյուրում: Վերականգնելով, ըստ հնարավորության, արձանագրության վնասված և անհետացած մասերը, կարդացվում է այսպես.

⌈ԵՍ.....⌉ԱՊԵՍՏ ՄԻԱԲԱՆԵՑԱ ⌈ՍՈՒՐԲ ՈՒԽ⌉ՏԻՍ ՎԱՆՔՍՏ/⌈ԱՆԱ
ԵՒ⌉ ԵՏՈՒ Ի ՀԱԼԱԼ ԱՐԴԵՆՑ ԻՄՈ(Յ) :Ի: ԴՀ (ԴԱՀԵԿԱՆ). ԵՒ /
ԳԼԽԱԻՈՐՔՍ ԽՈՍՏԱՑԱՆ Ի ՏԱՐԻՆ :Բ: ԺԱՄ Ի ՏԱՐԻՆ /
⌈ՏԵԱՌՆԸ⌉ՆԴԱՌԱՋԻՆ. ԿԱՏԱՐԻՉՔՆ ԱԻՐՀՆԻՆ ՅԱԼՍՏՈՒԾՈՅ:

Նկատողություն

Առաջին տողում նվիրատուի անվան միայն վերջն է պահպանվել. կարդացվում է ԱՂԵՍՏ կամ ԱՊԵՍՏ. գուցե անունը լինի Հայրապետ կամ Նահապետ (Ա2խ.Ք.):

32. Խաղ եպիսկոպոսի դամբանագիրը

Հարավային ապառաժից ներքև, ճանապարհի գլխին, կալի եզերքին, կան մի քանի քարեր, որոնցով իմիրզեկցիք հարբեցրել են տեղանքը կալ շինելու համար: Այստեղ գտնվեց մի շիրմաքար՝ քիչ կոտրված ծայրով (1,99 x 0,51 մ): Քարի մշակումը հասարակ է, տաշված է հարթ ու նույնիակ ունի փոքր ծռություն: Դրսի կողմի վրա քանդակազարդ պարզ շրջանակ ունի, որի մեջ, վերին մասում գծագրված է եպիսկոպոսական թագ, իսկ նրա տակ, քարի ամբողջ երկարությամբ՝ գավազան, որի երկու կողմերում գրված է արձանագրություն՝ երեք տողից.

ԱՅՍ Է ՀԱՆԿԻՍՏ /
ԽԱՂ ԵՊ(ԻՍԿՈՊՈՍԻ)[19]:

---

[19] Խաղ եպիսկոպոսը վկայված է 1560 թ. Վանստանի վանքում ընդօրինակված մի ձեռագրի հիշատակարանում որպես գրիչ (Գ.Հովսեփեան, Խաղբակեանք կամ Պոոշեանք Հայոց պատմութեան մեջ, հտ. Գ, Նիւ Եորք, 1942/3, էջ 125):

33-42. *Ten benefaction inscriptions*

On several nearby stones previously situated in one of the walls of the church were inscribed 10 different texts by different authors and with different subjects. Four of them were uncovered during our excavations just within the ruins of the church. One stone of quadrangle form (as well as many other stones from the monument) had been used by the villagers to level a hole in front of the church. We pulled it out and gathered all the stones to a place beside the table inside the church.[20] It then became clear that the initial number of stones with inscriptions was five, of which only four had been recovered: the first, third, fourth and fifth. The sizes of the first and third stones are similar (0.69 x 0.83 m); the size of the fourth is 0.69 x 0.56 m, and the size of the fifth is 0.69 x 0.37 m. The sizes of the letters are 6-7 cm. Reconstructing these inscriptions as much as possible (including the parts of the second missing stone), they read as shown on p. 41.[21]

Pl. 8:3; 9:1

---

[20] Only fragments of the first and third stones were found, in a wall of one of the houses of the village. Most of the stones uncovered during the excavations of 1912 were subsequently broken into fragments by the villagers and used in their constructions.

[21] Clearly the Umek and Turan mentioned in this inscription are the same two individuals mentioned in two inscriptions of Geghard, a religious centre located 15 km from Vanstan (G. Hovsepian, *op. cit.*, p. 48-49).

33-42. Տասը նվիրատվական արձանագրություն

Եկեղեցու պատերից մեկում, իրար կողքի շարված մի քանի քարերի վրա, խիտ ձևով, տեղի մեծ խնայողությամբ, տեղավորված են եղել մեկը մյուսի տակ 10 առանձին-առանձին արձանագրություններ՝ գրված տարբեր մարդկանց կողմից և վերաբերող այլ և այլ նվերների: Չորս քար այդ արձանագրությունների մասերով, մեկը մյուսից անկախ, բացվեցին մեր աշխատանքների ընթացքում անմիջապես եկեղեցու ավերակների վրա, որ գուցե մատնացույց է անում նրանց նախկին տեղը՝ եկեղեցու պատերի ներքին մասերում: Այդ քարերից մեկը, մոտավորապես քառակուսի, ըստ նախկին տեղի՝ առաջինը, ներկայիս բնակիչների կողմից օգտագործվել է այլ բազմաթիվ բեկորների հետ միասին՝ հարքելու համար այն թերությունը և փոսը, որ կան եկեղեցու հրապարակի և հարավային կողմի ապառաժի միջև: Այդտեղից քարը հանեցինք մեծ դժվարությամբ: Մյուս երեք քարերը պեղված են եկեղեցու ներսում: Ներկայումս դրանք շարքով դարսված են սեղանի առաջ՝ առաջինը սեղանին զուգահեռ, իսկ մյուս երեքը՝ ուղղահայաց ձևով նրա աջ կողմից[20]: Պարզվում է, որ արձանագրություններով քարերի թիվը եղել է հինգ: Դրանցից գտնված են միայն չորսը, որոնք շարքի մեջ զբաղեցրել են 1, 3, 4 և 5 տեղերը. պակասում է միայն երկրորդ քարը: Նրանց մեծությունը. առաջին քարի չափերը վրիպել են ուշադրությունից (բայց նա մոտավորապես հավասար է երրորդ քարին), երրորդինը՝ 0,69 x 0,83 մ, չորրորդինը՝ 0,69 x 0,56 մ, հինգերորդինը՝ 0,69 x 0,37 մ: Գրերի երկարությունը՝ 6-7 սմ: Վերականգնելով որքան որ հնարավոր է, կոտած (2-րդ) քարի մասերը ևս, արձանագրությունները իրենց ամբողջական ձևով կարդացվում են այսպես. յուրաքանչյուր արձանագրություն գրում եմ առանձին տողերում.

1. ԿԱՍԱՒՆ ԱՍՏՈՒԾՈՅ ԵՍ ՅՈՎԱՆԵՍ ⌈ԵՏՈՒ Ի ՍՈՒՐԲ ՈՒԽՏՍ ⌉Խ: ԴԱՀ(ԵԿԱՆ) ԵՒ Ե⌈ԴԲԱՐՔՍ ԳՐԵՑԻՆ ⌉Բ: ԺԱՄ Ի ՏԱՐԻ ՅՈՎԱՆՈՒ:
2. ԵՍ ՊԱԻՂՈՍ ԵՏՈՒ Ի ՍՈՒՐԲ ՈՒԽՏ⌈Ս ⌉Ի: ԴԱՀ(ԵԿԱՆ) / ԵՒ ՍՊԱՍԱԻՈՐՔ ՍՈՐ⌈Ա ԳՐԵՑԻՆ :Ա: ԺԱՄ ԻՆՉ:
3. ԵՍ ԳԼԽԱԹՈՒՆՍ ԵՏՈՒ :Ի: ԴԱՀ(ԵԿԱՆ)/ԵՒ ԳՐԵՑԻՆ ԻՆՉ :Ա: ԺԱՄ Ի ՏԱՐ⌈ՆԻ.....⌉
4. ԵՍ ՍԵԻԻԿԱ, ՄԱՍԵՐՍ ՏՎԱՔ ⌈:Խ: ԴԱՀԵԿԱՆ ԵՒ ԳՐԵՑԻՆ :Բ: ԱԻ⌉Ր ՊԱՏԱՐԱԳԵԼ ՄԵԶ ՉՔՐԻՍՏՈՍ:
5. ԵՍ ՄԵՐՉԵ 4.⌈ԵՍ .....Ս Ե⌉ՏՈՒ :Խ: ԴԱՀ(ԵԿԱՆ) ԵՒ ԳՐԵՑԻՆ ԻՆՉ :Բ: ԺԱՄ:
6. ԵՏՈՒ ⌈ՉԻՄ ԱՅԳԻՆ/ԿԵՍՆ ԽՈՒՊԱՆՈՎՆ Ի ՍԼՈՒՐԲՔՍ ԵՒ ԽՈՄ⌈ՏԱՑԱՆ ... ԺԱՄ. ՈՎ ԽԱՓԱՆԷ ՉԱՅԳԻՆ ԿԱՄ ՉԺԱՄ⌈Ն⌉.Յ.Ժ.Ք. ՀԱՅՐԱՊԵՏԱՅՆ ՆԶՈՎԱԾ Է:
7. ԵՍ ԽԱԹՈՒՆԻԿԱ ԵՏՈՒ :Ի:⌈ԴԱՀԵԿԱՆ ԵՒ ԳՐԵՑԻՆ ԻՆՉ :Ա:⌉ ԺԱՄ:
8. ՄԵՔ ԵՂԲԱՐՔՍ ՈՒՍԵԿ ԵՒ ԹՈՒՐԱՆՍ ՏՎԱՔ :Ծ: ԴԱՀԵԿ(ԱՆ) Ի ՍՈՒՐԲ ՈՒԽՏՍ. ԵՒ ԳՐԵՑԻՆ ⌈:Բ: ԺԱՄ.....⌉[21]:
9. ԵՍ ⌈..... ⌉ՔԱՂԱՔՍ ՏՎԻ :Խ: ԴԱՀ(ԵԿԱՆ) Ի ՍԼՈՒՐԲ ՈՒԽՏՍ ԵՒ ⌈ՍՊ⌉ԱՍԱԻՈՐՔՍ ՏՎԻՆ ԻՆՉ :Բ: ⌈ԺԱՄ:
10. ԵՍ ՍԱՐԳԻՍ ԵՒ ԱՄՈՒՍ⌈ԻՆ ԻՄ ...... ՏՈՒ⌈ՆՔ :Խ: ԴԱՀ(ԵԿԱՆ) ԵՒ ԳՐԵՑ⌈ԻՆ⌉ :Բ: ⌈ԺԱՄ⌉:

---

[20] Ներկայումս տեղում պահպանվել է հիշյալ չորս քարերից առաջինը և երրորդի երկու բեկորները, որոնք գտնվել են մեր կողմից մի տան պատի մեջ: Հուշարձանի շինաքարերի զգալի մասը 1912 թ. պեղումներից հետո տեղի բնակիչների կողմից կոտրվել է և շարվել գյուղի շինությունների պատերի մեջ:

[21] Ակներևաբար վիմագրում հիշատակված Ուսեկը և Թուրանը որպես նվիրատուներ վկայված են Գեղարդավանքի (XII-XIII դարերի ն՜անավոր վանական համալիր Վանստանից մոտ 15 կմ հյուսիս) երկու վիմագրերում (Գ.Հովսեփեան, Խաղբակեանք..., հտ. 3, էջ 48, 49):

43. *Inscription of Paul*

A quadrangle stone removed from one of the walls of barns to the west of the monument bears a six line inscription. The surface of the stone is badly damaged; the last two lines have suffered the most.

Pl. 9:2

Comment: After the word խափանէ a badly damaged two-line inscription is engraved. (H.M., G.S.)

44. *Benefactor inscription*

A small quadrangle stone (0.64 x 0.43 m) was found within the ruins of the church, in front of the table. It has 5 lines; the letter sizes are 5-6 cm.

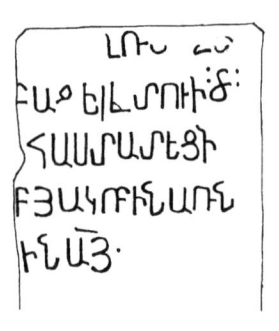

Pl. 10:1

Comments: This fragment shows that the inscription is incomplete both at the beginning and at the end. The missing parts were evidently on the adjacent stones (since this stone is complete). Although only one-third has survived, one can reconstruct the inscription almost completely. (Kalantar)

---

[22] Noragavith is a mediaeval town, presently in the suburbs of Erevan. It was renowned for its orchards.

43. Պողոսի արձանագրությունը

Մի քառանկյունի քար, որ հանվեց հուշարձանի արևմտյան կողմում շինված հարդանոցներից մեկի պատից, ունի 6 տող արձանագրություն։ Քարի երեսի կողմը քերված է և արձանագրությունը բավականաչափ վնասված, ամենից շատ վնասված են վերջին երկու տողերը։

ԿԱՄԱՒՆ ԱՅ ԵՍ ՄԵՂԱՊԱՐՏԵՍ ՊԱԻՂՈՍ / ՏՎԻ ԶԻՄ ՆՈՐԱՅ-
ԳԱԻԹՈՑ[22] ԱՅԳԻՆ ԵՒ ՄԻԱՅԲԱ / ՆԵՑԱՅ Ի ՍԼՈՒՐՔ ՈՒԽՏՍ ԵՒ
⌈ՍՊԱՍԱՒՈՐՔ⌉Ն ԳՐԵՑԻՆ ։Ժ։ ԺԱՄ Ի ՏԱՐ⌈ՈՒՄ ՅԵՏ⌉ ԻՄՈՅՆ
ՈՐ ԽԱՓԱՆԷ ⌈ԴԱՏԻ Ի ՏԵԱՌՆԷ⌉...։

Նկատողություն

Խափանէ բառից հետո, այլ տառաձևերով փորագրված է երկտող, համարյա ամբողջովին եղծված արձանագրություն (Հ.Մ., Գ.Ս.)։

44. Նվիրատվական արձանագրություն

Մի փոքրիկ քառանկյունի քար (0,64 x 0,43 մ), գտնված եկեղեցու ավերակների տեղում և դրված նրա սեղանի առաջ, ունի վնասված արձանագրություն՝ 5 տողից։ Գրերի երկարությունը՝ 5-6 սմ։

⌈ԿԱՄԱՒՆ ԱՅ ԵՍ ՄԵ⌈ՂՈՒՑ⌈ԵԱԼ⌉ Ծ⌈ԱՌԱՅՍ/.... ՄԻԱԲԱ-
ՆԵՑԱ ՍԼՈՒԻՐ⌉Ք ԱԾ⌈ԱԾՆԻՍ⌉ ԵՒ ՏՈՒԻ ։Ծ։ /⌈ԴԱՀԵԿԱՆ
ԵՒ ՍՊԱՍԱՒՈՐՔ ՍՈՐԱ⌉ ՀԱՍՏԱՏԵՑԻՆ /⌈։Բ։ ԱԻՐ
ՊԱՏԱՐԱԳ Ի ՏԱՐԻ ՍԼՈՒԻՐՔ⌉ ՅԱԿՈԲԻՆ ԱՌՆ /⌈ԵԼ.
ԿԱՏԱՐԻՉՔՆ ԱԻՐՀՆԻՆ ՅԱՍՏՈՒԾՈՅ։

Նկատողություն

Արձանագրության այս մնացորդի բովանդակությունից երևում է, որ այն թերի է տողերի թե սկզբից և թե վերջից։ Պակասող մասերը անշուշտ, եղել են հարևան քարերի վրա՝ երկու կողքերից (քանի որ մնացած քարն ինքն ամբողջ է)․ ուրեմն արձանագրությունը տեղավորված է եղել երեք քարերի վրա։ Չնայած պահպանված է նրա 1/3 մասը, այնուամենայնիվ նա վերականգնվում է իր նախկին ձևով, համարյա ամբողջությամբ (Աշխ.Ք.)։

---

[22] Միջնադարյան հայտնի բնակավայր, ներկայումս Երևանի արվարձան։ Հայտնի է եղել իր պտղատու այգիներով։

45. On the surviving western wall of the church, near its southern corner, just above the stairs in the rock, in pink color and in big letters, is written the following:

֎վ֊ ՊԼԳ֊․․

46. On one of the cornerstones of the monument, which was found on the south-eastern slope, above the road, a cross is engraved along with the letters:

ԲՐԱ

Inscriptions on khachkars (cross-stones). Most of the following were excavated from the ruins of barns built on the ruins of the monument, to the west and south of the church.

47. The khachkar of Amirze

Excavated on the north-eastern slope, above the road, the sixth in the row of khachkars (height: 1.17 m). On its upper side, on top of the cross, is a five-line inscription:

ԵՍԱՄԻՐՁ	ԱԿՆԵՅԻՍԻ
ՆՇԱՆՍԻԿԱ	ԵՍԱՄԵՐՈՐԴ
ԻՄՈՔԱՆՈՆ	ԻՔՈՒՐՁԻՆ
ԹԻՍ։Պ	
ՉԱ	

Pl. 10:3

48. Small khachkar (0.90 x 0.55 m), the second in the row of khachkars (close to the big khachkar erected near the rock). The main cross also has small crosses in four corners. Although the upper edge is broken, the inscription is legible:

․․․ԱՁ․․ԵՒԵ․․ԳԵԼՐ․․Ն

---

[23] The words ԻՄՈ ՔԱՆՈՆ Ի ՔԱՈՒՐՁԻՆ in the third line are unclear. Possibly to be reconstructed: ՈՐԴՈ ԻՄ ՈՒՔԱՆՈՅՆ Ի ՔԱՈՒՐԹԻՆ.

45. *Տաճարի մնացորդի արևմտյան պատի վրա*, նրա հարավային անկյան մոտ, ժայռից կերտված սանդուղքների հենց վերևում, գրված է վարդագույն ներկով, խոշոր գրերով.

ԹՎԻՆ] ՊԼԳ (1384 թ.):

46. *Հուշարձանի անկյունաքարերից մեկի վրա*, որ գտնվեց հարավ-արևելյան կողմի լանջում, ճանապարհի տակ: Մի երեսին քանդակված է խաչ և նրա կողքին գրված.

ՔԱՐԱՄ:

Արձանագրություններ խաչքարերի վրա

Մեծ մասամբ հանգված են հուշարձանի ավերակների վրա շինված հարդանոցների և գոմերի հասարակ պատերի միջից, կարգով դրված են մի շարք, տաճարի արևմտյան պատի առաջ եղած հրապարակում, նրա հարավային կողմում:

47. *Ամիրգեի խաչքարը*, բարձրությունը 1,17 մ, պեղված է հյուսիս-արևելյան լանջում, ճանապարհի գլխին և գրաղեցնում է 6-րդ տեղը խաչքարերի շարքում: Շրջանակի վերին մասում և խաչի գլխին ունի 5 տող արձանագրություն.

ԵՍ ԱՄԻՐՋ⌈ԵՍ Կ⌉ԱԿՆԵՑԻ ՍՒՈՒՐԲ /

ՆՇԱՆՍ ՅԻՇԱ⌈ՏԱ⌉Կ ԿԵՍԱՒՐԵԱ

ՈՐԴՈ⌈ՅՆ⌉/ ԻՄՈ ՔԱՆՈՆ Ի

ՔԱՈՒՉԻՆ[23] ԹԻՍ ։ՊՁԱ (1432 թ.):

48. *Փոքրադիր խաչքար* (0,90 x 0,55 մ), խաչքարերի շարքում դրված է երկրորդ տեղում (ապառաժի մոտ կանգնած խոշոր խաչքարի մոտ): Բացի մեծ խաչից ունի նաև մեկական մանր խաչեր չորս անկյուններում. վերին եզերքը ջարդոտված է, բայց և այնպես կարդացվում է.

⌈ՍՒՈՒՐԲ ԽԱՉ⌉Ս ԲԱՐԵ⌈ԽԱՒՍ Է ԳԱՒՍԱՐ ....Ն:

---

[23] Արձանագրության երրորդ տողում ԻՄՈ ՔԱՆՈՆ Ի ՔԱՈՒՉԻՆ բառակապակցությունը անհասկանալի է: Կարծում ենք, որ այստեղ կարելի է վերծանել ՈՐԴՈ ԻՄ ՈՒՔԱՆՈՅՆ Ի ՔԱՈՒԻԹԻՆ: Առաջարկվող վերծանությունը պայմանական է:

49. *The khachkar of Mr. Shrvanish and David*

The fourth in the row of khachkars (1.06 x 0.61 m), with an engraved rope-like frame. Two crosses are situated under the wings of the main cross, which are connected by an ornament. The two-line inscription is located at the upper edge, while the date is on the wings of the cross, again in two lines.

ՄԲ ԽՉ ԲՐԽՍԱՌԱԾՎԱՍ
ՊՐՇՐՎԱՆԻՇԻՆ ՊՐԴԱՒԻԹԻՆ
Թ   ՉԽ
Վ   Ը

50. *The khachkar of the priest Hovhannes*

The fifth in the row of khachkars (1.05 x 0.61 m). In style it is similar to the previous one: the inscription is on the upper edge, the date is on the wings:

ՄԲ ԽՉ ԲՐԵԽՍԱՌԱԾ
ՎԱՅՀԵՍՔՀԻՆՓԿԱԿԱԼ
Չ
Խ   ԹՎ
Ը

51. *Khachkar*

Found on the rock, above the khachkars (1.35 x 0.37 m), it is covered by a rich, fine sculpture. The date is engraved on the cross.

ԹՉԾՉ

---

[24] Mr. Shrvanish is mentioned by the priest Galust in his comments on the bible recopied in 1460 in the Aghjotz St. Stephanos church (XVth century Armenian comments, part 3 (1481-1500), compiled by L.S. Khachikyan, Erevan 1967, p. 435).

[25] ՓԱԿԱԿԱԼ mentioned in the inscription is a religious degree in the Armenian church (*New Dictionary of Armenian Language* 2, p. 24-25, Venice, 1837).

THE INSCRIPTIONS OF VANSTAN

49. Պարոն Շրվանիշի և Դավթի խաչքարը

Դրված է խաչքարերի շարքի երրորդ տեղում (1,06 x 0,61 մ), ոտք չունի, շրջանակը պարանանման հյուսվածքով: Խաչի քերի տակ երկու փոքր խաչեր միացած են հյուսանման քանդակով: Արձանագրությունը՝ 2 տողից, բռնում է վերին եզերքը, իսկ թվականը՝ խաչի քերի վրա, նույնպես 2 տող:

Ս[ՈՒՐ]Բ Խ[ԱՉՍ] Բ[ԱՐ]ԵԽ[Ա]Յ ԱՌ ԱԾ /

ՎԱ[ՍՆ] ՊԱ[ՐՈՆ] ՇՐՎԱՆԻՇԻՆ[24],

ՊԱ[Ր]Ո[Ն] ԴԱԻԹԻՆ / ԹՎԻ[Ն] :ՋԽԸ: (1499 թ.):

50. Հովհաննես քահանայի խաչքարը

Դրված է խաչքարերի շարքի հինգերորդ տեղում (1,05 x 0,61 մ), իր գեղարվեստական մշակությամբ միանգամայն նման է նախորդ խաչքարին: Արձանագրությունը վերին եզերքում է, իսկ թվականը՝ խաչի քերի վրա.

Ս[ՈՒՐ]Բ Խ[Ա]Չ[Ս] Բ[ԱՐ]ԵԽ[Ա]Յ ԱՌ ԱԾ /

ՎԱ[ՍՆ] ՅՈՀ[ԱՆ]ԷՍ Ք[Ա]Հ[Ա] ՆԱՅԻՆ

Փ[Ա]ԿԱԿԱԼ[25] / ԹՎԻ[Ն] ՋԽԸ (1499 թ.):

51. Խաչքար

Գտնվում է հիշված խաչքարերի վերևում, ապառաժի վրա, թեք կերպով պառկած (1,35 x 0,37 մ). ծածկված է նուրբ հարուստ քանդակով: Խաչանշանի վերևում գրված է միայն թվականը.

ԹՎԻ[Ն] ՋԾՋ (1507 թ.):

---

[24] Պարոն Շրվանիշը հիշված է 1460 թ. Գալուստ արքեպայի կողմից Աղցոց Սուրբ Ստեփանոս վանքում ընդօրինակված Ավետարանի հիշատակարանում (ԺԵ դարի հայերեն հիշատակարաններ, մասն 3 (1481-1500 թթ.), կազմեց Լ.Ս.Խաչիկյան, Երևան, 1967, էջ 435):

[25] Եկեղեցական պաշտոն, «Ունող զիակական դրան՝ իշխանութբ բանալոյ և փակելոյ, պետ բանալեաց, գլխավոր դռնապան, եկեղեցպան, լուսարար» (Նոր բառգիրք Հայկազեան լեզուի, հտ. 2, Վենետիկ, 1837, էջ 24-25):

52. Khachkar

The seventh in the row, near the khachkar of Amirze (both were excavated in the same place); 0.95 x 0.48 m. Has a two-line damaged inscription:

ՅԱՆԵՅԱ֊ ՓՐԿՈՒՂ
ՀՈԳՈՅ ԱՍՆՅԻՔ

ԹՎ ՈՒՁ

Pl. 10:2

Comments: In the first line of the inscription after the word ԿԱԿՆԵՑԱԻ the remnants of letters are visible and can be restored as ԽԱՉՍ. Below the date is the following: ԹՎ ՊՁ (1431). (H.M., G.S.)

53. Khachkar of Martiros

On the khachkar situated on the simple wall to the north-west of the monument is written:

ՄԲ ԽԱՉՍԱԳՆԱԿԱՆԷ ․Տ․ ՈՍԻՆ

54. Khachkar of Mirze

In the wall of a house in the village, to the west of the monument, a khachkar (1.47 x 0.76 m) with the following inscription was found:

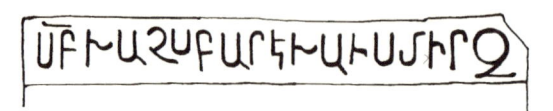

ՄԲ ԻԱՇՍԲԱՐԽԱՍՄԻՐՁ

52. *Խաչքար*

Խաչքարների շարքում, 7-րդ տեղում, Ամիրգեի խաչքարի կողքին (երկուսն էլ պեղված են մի տեղում) (0,95 x 0,48 մ)։ Քիվին ունի 2 տող արձանագրություն՝ վնասված մասերով։

⸢Կ⸣ԱԿՆԵՑԱԻ ⸢ՆՇԱՆՍ⸣ ՓՐԿՈՒԹԵԱՆ⸣/
ՀՈԳՈՑ Թ...ԱՏԻՆ. ՅԻՇ⸢ԵՑԵՔ ԻՅ ՔՐԻՍՏՈՍ⸣։

Նկատողություն

Արձանագրության առաջին տողում, ԿԱԿՆԵՑԱԻ բառից հետո նկատվում են տառերի հետքեր, որոնք վերծանվում են ԽԱՉՍ։ Քիվից ներքև փորագրված է թվականը՝ ԹՎ ՊՁ (1431 թ.) (Հ.Մ., Գ.Ս.)։

53. *Մարտիրոսի խաչքարը*

Հուշարձանը հյուսիս-արևմտյան կողմից շրջապատող հասարակ պարսպի արտաքին մուտքի մոտ դրված խաչքարի վրա կարդացվում է։

Ս⸢ՈՒՐ⸣Բ ԽԱՉՍ ԱԻԳՆԱԿԱՆ Է ⸢ՄԱՐ⸣Տ⸢ԻՐ⸣ՈՍԻՆ։

54. *Սիրգեի խաչքարը*

Հուշարձանի արևմտյան հրապարակի վրա նայող *գյուղական մի շենքի* պատի մեջ, դրսի կողմից դրված է մի *խաչքար* (1,47 x 0,76 մ), որի վրա կարդացվում է։

Ս⸢ՈՒՐ⸣Բ ԽԱՉՍ ԲԱՐԵԽԱՒՍ Լ⸢Է⸣ ՍԻՐՉ⸢ԻՆ⸣։

55. Khachkar of Simeon

Was found to the north of the monument, near the north-east corner of the western wall, in front of the entrance of the fence. The inscription is under the cross:

ԲԱՐՇԵԱՋՍԻՄԷՈՆԲՈԴԱԼԸՍ
ՏԵԱՆԴ

56. Inscription on the tomb

A grave-stone was excavated in the threshing floor to the north of the monument. On the right of it is a roughly engraved, standing, bearded human figure (length: 1.15 m; width: 0.28 m) with his hands on his chest. To the left is a sculpture showing three small crosses under arches, with a one-line inscription on the upper part:

ԱՅԱՀԱՆԳԻՍՏՏՐ··· ԹՈ

57. Khachkar

Uncovered on the eastern slope, below the road (0.85 x 0.48 m), with a one-line inscription above the frame and a date below the cross:

Pl. 10:4

55. Սիմէոնի խաչքարը

Գտնված հուշարձանի հյուսիսային կողմում և դրված արևմտյան պատի հյուսիս-արևմտյան անկյան մոտ, շրջապարսպի մուտքի դիմաց: Արձանագրությունը փորագրված է խաչի տակ.

Ք[ՐԻՍՏՈ]Ս ՀԻՇԵԱ ՁՍԻՄԷՈՆ [Ի] ՔՈ

ԳԱԼՍՏ / ՏԵԱՆԴ:

56. Արձանագրություն տապանաքարի վրա

Գերեզմանատարածան, որ պեղվեց կալի մեջ, հուշարձանի հյուսիսային կողմում և դրվեց մյուս բեկորների հետ, արևմտյան պատի մոտ: Աջ կողմի վրա ունի կոպիտ մշակված մի նկար՝ մարդու ամբողջ հասակով, ձեռքերը խաչաձև ծալած կրծքին, մորուքով (նկարի երկարությունը՝ 1,15 մ, լայնքը՝ ուսերում՝ 0,28 մ): Արձանի ձախ կողի վրա քանդակ է՝ երեք մանր խաչեր իրար միացած կամարների տակ, իսկ վերին երեսի վրա ունի մի տող արձանագրություն.

ԱՅՍ Է ՀԱՆԳԻՍՏ Տ[ԷՐ] ... [ԻՆ]. ԹՎԻՆ] Ռ (1551 թ.):

57. Խաչքար

Ընկած է արևելյան լանջին, ճանապարհից ցած, եկեղեցու հյուսիս-արևելյան անկյունից ուղիղ գծի վրա (0,85 x 0,48 մ), ունի իր շրջանակի վերին մասում գրված մի տող, իսկ խաչի տակ՝ թվականը.

Ս[ՈՒՐ]Բ ԽԱ[Չ]Ս ԲԱՐԵԽԱՍ [Է] Ն...ԱՍԻՆ /

ԹՎԻՆ] ՌԺԵ (1566 թ.):

58. Khachkar

On the inner side of the western wall of the mosque in the village was found a small inscribed khachkar.

ՄԽԱՉԹԽԱԽԱՌ
ԱԾՊՆ ԱՌԱԶ
ՈԱՀՆ...

59. Khachkar of Mr. Tajer

Near a house to the north-east of the monument, a khachkar with the following inscription was found:

ՄԲ ԽԱՉՍԲԱԼԵԽԱՍ ՊՐ ԹԶԵՐԻՆ

60. Khachkar

In the wall surrounding the monument, on the west, near its southern corner, this khachkar with an inscription was found. Since it was turned to the inside, only the following could be read:

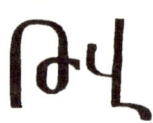

ԹՎ

61. Khachkar

Situated 15 m north of the church, in the north wall of a small village house, was a khachkar bearing an inscription that was not readable because it was turned to the inside.

---

[26] 'Araj' is a rare name (1455?). In the comments to the bible recopied in Aspaveruk village, the father of the patron, Mrs. Dshkhuhi, is mentioned as Mr. Araj (XVth Century Armenian Manuscripts, Part II (1451-1480, L.S. Khatchikian, Erevan, 1958).

[27] G. Hovsepian (Part I, Vagharshapat 1928, p. 66), who first published this inscription, identified Mr. Tajer with the wife of Amir-Hasan, a member of the Khaghbakian or Proshian dynasty.

58. Խաչքար

Գյուղի մզկիթի գավթի արևմտյան պատի ներքին մասում գտնվում է ոչ մեծ մի *խաչքար*, որի վրա, խաչի տակ, գրված է.

ՍԸՈՒՐԲ ԽԱՉ[Ս] ԲԱՐԵԽԱԻՍ ԱՌ / ԱԾ ՊԱՐՈՆ

ԱՌԱճ[26]... / ՌԱՀՆ...:

59. Պարոն Թաճերի խաչքարը

Ընկած է հուշարձանի հյուսիս-արևելյան կողմում, մի տան մոտ, քիվին փորագրված է.

ՍԸՈՒՐԲ ԽԱՉՍ ԲԱՐԵԽԱԻՍ [Է] ՊլԱյՐլՈՆյ ԹլԱյճԵՐԻՆ[27]:

60. Խաչքար

Հուշարձանը արևմտյան կողմից շրջափակող հասարակ պատի մեջ, նրա հարավ-արևմտյան անկյունում, դրված է մի խաչքար, որն ունի արձանագրություն: Սակայն այդ երեսով նա դարձած լինելով դեպի ներս, կարդացվում է միայն.

ԹՎ

61. Խաչքար

Գտնվում է տաճարից 15 քայլի վրա, դեպի հյուսիս, մի ցածր գյուղական տան հյուսիսային պատի մեջ. Նույնպես ունի արձանագրություն: Սակայն շրջված է երեսի վրա և հնարավոր չէ կարդալ:

---

[26] Հազվագյուտ անձնանվանակերտ արմատ: 1455 թ.? Ասպավերուկ գյուղում ընդօրինակված մի Ավետարանի հիշատակարանում որպես ձեռագրի պատվիրատու Տիկին Դշխոի հայր վկայված է պարոն Առաջը (Ժէ դարի հայերեն ձեռագրերի հիշատակարաններ, մաս Բ (1451-1480 pp.), կազմեց Լ.Ս.Խաչիկյան, Երևան, 1958):

[27] Արձանագրության առաջին հրատարակիչ Գ.Հովսեփյանը պարոն Թաճերին իրավացիորեն նույնացնում է միջնադարյան Հայաստանի նշանավոր Խոդրակյան կամ Պոշյան իշխանական տան ներկայացուցիչ Ամիր-Հասանի կնոջ՝ Թաճերի հետ (Գ.Հովսեփյան, Խոդրակյանք..., մաս1, Վաղարշապատ, 1928, էջ 66):

62. South of the monument, near the road, in the wall of a cattle shed, was found a processed stone upon which, below three crosses, the following was written in capital and small letters:

$$\text{Ած որրմի գաոն քաք ---}$$

63. On a quadrangle stone covered by half-circles, with false arches and crosses, located near the western wall of the monument, in front of the stairs, we read:

$$\text{Մբ խչս Բրխաս}$$

4. INSCRIPTIONS FROM THE SURROUNDINGS OF VANSTAN[28]

64. In the Hermit's Cave, above the inner entrance, on both sides of the cross is written:

$$\text{ԱՅՐՁԳՆԱՎՈՒՐ}$$

65. *The inscription of Sargis (1282)*

On the road from Vanstan to Gyolaysor, below the village of Kyopri-Kulakh, on a smoothed surface of a huge rock, is engraved a cross within double circles, resembling a khachkar both in its size and its processing. On the frame of the cross-stone an inscription of Sargis and Musnurmatin is engraved, in seven lines with large capital letters:

---

[28] In his original work on the inscriptions of Vanstan, A. Kalantar included four inscriptions found in the vicinity of that site, not directly related to it, but having an important content.

62. Հուշարձանից հարավ, ճանապարհի մոտ, *գոմի պատի մեջ* կա մի քար, մշակված երեսով դարձած դեպի դուրս, որի վրա, երեք մեծ ու փոքր խաչանշանների տակ գրված է անցողական (գլխագրից-փոքրատառի) գրով.

ԱԾ ՈՂՈՐՄԻ ՊԱՐՈՆ ԲԱԲ...⌈ԻՆ⌉:

63. Մի *քառանկյուն անկյունաքար*՝ զարդարված կիսաշրջաններով, կեղծ կամարներով և խաչանշաններով, գտնվում է հուշարձանի արևմտյան պատի մոտ, սանդուղքների առաջ, ունի գրություն՝ բոլորագրով.

ՍՈՒՐ|Բ ԽԱՉՍ Բ|ԱՐԵ|ԽԱ|ԻՍ...:

4. Վանստանի շրջակայքի արձանագրությունները[28]

64. «*Ճգնավորի այր*»-ի մեջ, ներսի մուտքի գլխին, խաչանշանի երկու կողմերում գրված է.

ԱՅՐ ՃԳՆԱՎՈՒՐ:

65. *Սարգսի արձանագրությունը (1282թ.)*

Իմիրզեկ գյուղից դեպի Գյուլայտոր տանող ճանապարհի վրա, Քյուֆրի կուլախ գյուղից ներքև, մի հկայական մեծության *ժայռաբեկորի* հարթեցված մակերեսին փորված է մի խաչ՝ կրկնակի շրջանակի մեջ, որը թե չափով և թե մշակությամբ նման է խաչքարի: Այդ խաչքարի շրջանակի վրա չորսջանակի գրված է Սարգսի և Մուսնուրմատինի արձանագրությունը, 7 տող խոշոր գլխագրերով.

---

[28] Աշխ.Քալանթարը սույն ժողովածուի մեջ ներառել է նաև շրջակա հուշարձաններից հավաքած ևս չորս արձանագրություն, որոնք, չնայած, անմիջականորեն չեն առնչվում Վանստանի հետ, սակայն ունեն աղբյուրագիտական կարևոր նշանակություն:

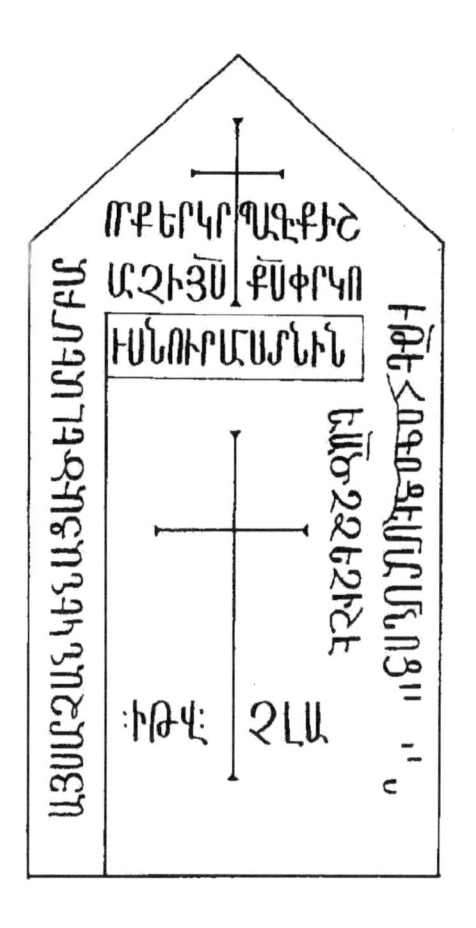

Pl. 11:1

Comment: We present an alternative reconstruction, which presumably more correctly reflects the content and the structure of the inscription:

"MUSNURMATIN", which is an unknown name, can be split into ՄՍՈՒՄՆՈ ԻՐ ՍԱՍՏՆԻՆ. The letter Մ might be confused with Ա, and Ս was overlooked after the letters ՍԱ. (H.M., G.S.)

66. Grave-stone inscription

In the village of Kyopri-Kulakh, near the small ruined basilica, a double-sided grave-stone with a four-line inscription was found. Because of the style of the grave-stone and the archaeological peculiarities of the inscription, both can be attributed to the X-XIth centuries:

ԱՅՍ ԱՐՁԱՆ ԿԵՆԱՑ ԱԽԵԼԱյԼ ԱՐԵԱՄԲ

ԱՐԱՐՉԻ ՈՐՔ ԵՐԿՐՊԱԳԷՔ

ՅԻՇԵՑԵՔ ի] ՅԻՍՈՒՅՍ ՔՐԻՍՏՈյՍ

ՓՐԿՈՒԹԵԼԱՆյ ՀՈԳՈՑ ԵՒ ՄԱՐՄՆՈՑ

ՍԱՐԳՍԻ ԵՒ ՄՈՒԽՆՈՒՐՍԱՏԻՆ ԵՒ

Ա͞Ծ ՁՁԵՁ ՅԻՇ։ Ի ԹՎԻՆյ .ՉԼԱ

(1282թ.):

Նկատողություն

Ստորև առաջարկում ենք այս արձանագրության՝ տողանջատման այլ սկզբունքով կատարված վերծանությունը, որը, կարծում ենք, առավել ճիշտ է բնորոշում վիմագրի բովանդակությունն ու կառուցվածքը.

ԱՅՍ ԱՐՁԱՆ ԿԵՆԱՑ ԱԽԵԱԼ ԱՐԵԱՄԲ ԱՐ / ԱՐՉԻ Յ͞Ս Ք͞Ս Ի ՓՐԿՈ / ԻԹԵԻՒՆ
ՀՈԳՈՑ ԵՒ ՄԱՐՄՆՈՑ ՍԱՐԳՍԻ ԵՒ ԱՄՈ/ԽՄՆՈ ԻՒՐ ՄԱԱՏՆԻՆ / ՈՐՔ
ԵՐԿՐՊԱԳԷՔ ՅԻՇ[Է]ՑԵՔ ԵՒ Ա͞Ծ ՁՁԵՁ ՅԻՇ. / Ի ԹՎԻՆ] ՉԼԱ (1282թ.):

ՄՈՒԽՆՈՒՐՍԱՏԻՆ անհասկանալի և անձանոթ անձնանվան ճիշտ բառանջատման շնորհիվ այն վերծանվում է ՄԱՈՒՄՆՈ ԻՒՐ ՄԱՍՏՆԻՆ։ Առաջին Մ տառի վրա չի նկատվել Ա-ի փոքր աստղը, իսկ վերջում՝ ՄԱ կցագրից հետո Ս տառը (Հ.Մ., Գ.Ս.):

66. Արձանագրություն տապանաքարի վրա

Իմիրզեկի հարևան Քյոփրի կուլախ գյուղում ավերակացած փոքրիկ բազիլիկայի մոտ կա մի երկթեք գերեզմանաքարձան, որի վրա գրված է չորս տող արձանագրություն։ Գերեզմանա-քարձանն ըստ տիպի, և արձանագրությունն ըստ իր հնագրական առանձնահատկությունների՝ կարող է վերագրվել X-XI դդ.

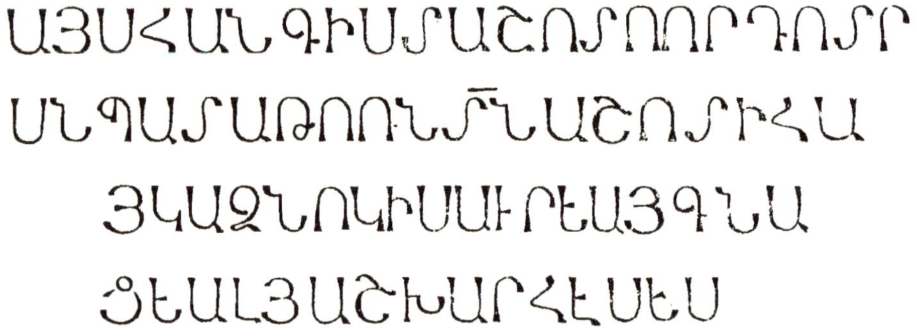

ԱՅՍՀԱՆԳԻՍՏԱՇՈՐՈՐԴՈՑՐ
ՍՊԱՄԱԹՈՒՆՄՆԱՇՈՐԻՀԱ
ՅԿԱՉՆՈԻԿԻՍԱԻՐԵԱՅԳՆԱ
ԾԵԱԼՅԱՇԽԱՐՀԵՍԵՍ

Pl11:2a

Comments: The first line of the inscription is damaged and therefore hardly legible. The word ՀԱՆԳԻՍՏ can also be read as ՀԱՆԳՍՏԱՐԱՆ. The last letters ԵՍ might constitute the beginning of a new phrase (Kalantar).

The inscription is engraved on both faces of the stone. In 1912, the grave-stone was presumably still half in the earth, and therefore Kalantar perhaps did not notice the additional four lines. Thus the whole inscription has nine line

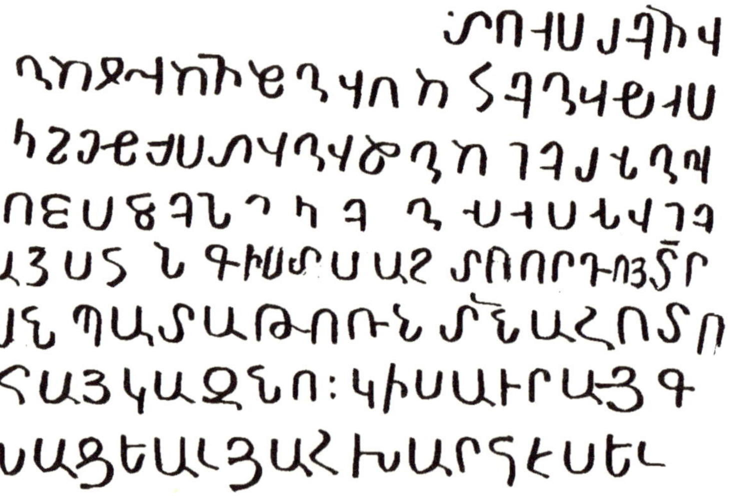

Pl. 11:2a, b

By their character, the names mentioned in this inscription indicate their probable attribution to one of the renowned Armenian princes dynasties. The Bagratunis can be excluded, however, since in their inscriptions the family name is always mentioned. Such names are often met in inscriptions of the dynasty of the "Haykazun" princes of Syunik, although this can not be assumed as certain, since it was not possible to locate them in any historical source (H.M., G.S.).

ԱՅՍ ՀԱՆԳԻՍՏ [Է] ԱՇՈՏՈ, ՈՐԴՈ Տ[ԷՐ] / ՍՆՊԱՏԱ, ԹՈՌՆ Տ[ԵԱՌ]Ն
ԱՇՈՏԻ / ՀԱՅԿԱԶՆՈ ԿԻՍԱԻՐԵԱՅ Գ/ՆԱՑԵԱԼ ՅԱՇԽԱՐՀԷՍ ԵՍ...:

Նկատողություն

Արձանագրության առաջին տողը եղծված է և վատ է կարդացվում, ՀԱՆԳԻՍՏ, կարող է կարդացվել և ՀԱՆԳՍՏԱՐԱՆ: Վերջում գրված է ԵՍ, որ թվում է ավելորդ, կամ գուցե մի նոր պարբերության սկիզբ է, որը չի ավարտվել, մնացել է կիսատ (Ա₂խ.Ք.):

Նկատողություն

Արձանագրությունը փորագրված է երկյանց տապանաքարի երկու նիստերին (առաջին տողը լանջերի հատման հատվածում): Տապանաքարը, հավանաբար, 1912թ. կիսով չափ թաղված է եղել հողի մեջ և Ա₂խ.Քալանթարը չի նկատել մյուս նիստին փորագրված շարունակության չորս տողերը: Ամբողջ արձանագրությունը ինը տողից է:

ԱՅՍ ՀԱՆԳԻՍՏՍ ԱՇ[Ո]ՏՈ, ՈՐԴՈՑ Տ͞Ր / ՍՆՊԱՏԱ, ԹՈՌՆ Տ͞Ն ԱՇՈՏՈ /
ՀԱՅԿԱԶՆՈ: ԿԻՍԱԻՐ[Ե]ԱՅ Գ/ՆԱՑԵԱԼ ՀԱՇԽԱՐՀԷՍ ԵԻ/ԵԼ Ի ԴՈՒՌՆ
ԵԿԵՂԵՑՈՅՍ / ԽՆԴՐԵԼ ԱՆՁԻՆ ԻՄՈ ԲԺՇԿ/ՈՒԹԻՆ ԵՀԱՄ ԻՆՉ ՎԱՆՃԱՆ
Ի ՎԵՐՈՒՍ:

Արձանագրության մեջ հիշատակված անձնանուններից և պատվանուններից (Հայկազուն, տեր) դատելով, վկայված անձինք պատկանել են Հայաստանի նշանավոր իշխանական տներից մեկին: Բագրատունյաց տոհմին պատկանելը բացառվում է, քանի որ նրանց անունից փորագրված վիմագրերում մշտապես նշվում են տոհմանունը կամ թագավորական ծագումը: Այս անունները հաճախ են հանդիպում Սյունյաց գահերեց «Հայկազուն» իշխանների տոհմածառում: Նշված անձանց Սյունյաց իշխանական տոհմին պատկանելը չենք կարող վերջնական համարել, քանի որ սկզբնաղբյուրներում այդ մասին ուղղակի վկայություններ չեն պահպանվել (Հ.Մ., Գ.Ս.):

67. *The inscription of the queen Khosrovanuysh*

In the village of Kyopri-Kulakh, near the same ruined basilica, the inscription of the queen Khosrovanuysh is engraved in 10 lines close to each other, and with unequal letters:[29]

ՆՀԵՐԹՈՒՅԱՆՈՒՆ ԱՅԵՍԽՈՄՐՈՎԱՆՈՅԶԹ ԱԴՈՒՀ
ԻԱՉԱՏԷՅԻՉՄԱՆԿԱՆՑ ՀԱԻՅԱՏՍՎԱՍՆ ԱՀՈՐՈՅԱՐ ԵՒՀ
ԱՄՈՒԹԵԱՆԵՒ ՎԷՐՈՒԴԵԱՅՍ ԴՀԱԵՒՍՄԲԱՏԱ = ԵՒԿԵՄԱՅԻ
ՆԵՒԱՄԼՉԱՅՍԹՈՒԵՂԵՒԱՀՍՈՂԱՅՆՂ ԴՈՒՀԱԿՈՒԱԿԿԱԱՅ
ՍԳՈՍԿԱԹ ԼՈՒԱՌԴՆ ԿԱԱՉԱՐ ԿԱՍԱՈՒՆՉՈՎԵԱԼԷՂՒՅԻՅԱ
ԼՑՆԱԿԱԼԵՆԱՅԵՒԵՐԵՐՐ:ՅՀԸ:ՀԱՄԱՊԵՄԱՅՆ ԿԱՊԵԱԼԷ
ՂԻՅՀՈԳՈՎԵՒՍԱՍՈՎԵԻԲԱԴՐԱՏՈՒԱ ՉԴԵԼԱՅՆՄՐԷ
ՂԻՅԻԱՐԱՉԻՄՅՍԿԿՍ ԱԻՉՔՀՐԱՆԱՅՏՈՑԱՀՐՆԵԱԼԷՉ
ԵՍԴՐԵՅԻՍԱԹԵՈՍԻԱՅՆԿԵԱՅԱՄՐ
ԱՆԵՑԻՍ

Comments: The date of the inscription, 1029, is legible, but it does not match the content of the inscription, i.e. the time of Khosrovanuysh.

Even if we read Լ instead of Հ (939), it is still not suitable; the letter Հ is probably an error, one should have Ճ (963). [36]

Seventh line: ՍԱՐՍՈՎ is written instead of ՍԱՐՄՆՈՎ.

Ninth line: ՍԻԱՅՆԿԱԵՅՍ instead of ՍԻԱՅՆԱԿԵՅՍ.

Fifth line: ԳՐՈՍ instead of ԳՐՈՅՍ (Kalantar).

---

[29] This stone was later removed, and at present is situated 10 km south-west of Vanstan in the cemetery of Gyolaysor village.
[30] An Armenian queen Khosrovanuysh and her husband, king Ashot III Voghormatz, engaged in considerable constructional activity; in particular, they founded the Sanahin church in 966.
[31] Shariat-tax payed to the landowner equal to 1/10 of the harvest (*History of the Armenian Nation* 3, Erevan, 1976, p. 258-259.
[32] Gagik I: Armenian king of the Bagratuni dynasty (990-1020).
[33] Smbat II Tiezerakal: Armenian Bagratuni king (977-990).
[34] According to the chronicles, king Ashot III Voghormatz and queen Khosrovanuysh had three sons, Smbat, Gagik and Gurgen. The latter became the founder of Tashir-Dzoraget kingdom and adopted the name Kyurike I. It is uncertain whether king Ashot and Khosrovanuysh also had a daughter named Keta.
[35] Matheos is the name of the scribe. Such a name is not mentioned in any other inscription. Matheos Taronatzi was a notable early scribe.
[36] The present reconstruction of this inscription by A.Kalantar was published by S. Avagian (*op. cit,* p. 283-287) in a discussion of the word 'SALUK', also mentioned here. Avagian dates the inscription to 959.

67. Խոսրովանույշ թագուհու արձանագրությունը

Քյուֆրի կուլախ գյուղում, միևնույն ավերակած բագիլիկայի մոտ, գտնվում է Խոսրովանույշ թագուհու արձանագրությունը՝ 10 տող, գրված տողերն իրար մոտիկ և անհավասար գրերով[29]:

ՆՀ ԵՒ Ը ԹՈՒ. ՅԱՆՈՒՆ ԱՅ ԵՍ ԽՈՍՐՈՎԱՆՈՅՇ ԹԱԳՈՒՀ/Ի[30] ԱԶԱՏԵՑԻ ԶՄԱՆԿԱՆՑ ՇԱՐԻՅԱՏՍ[31] ՎԱՄՆ ԱՇՏՈՑ ԱՐԵԻՇ / ԱՏՈՒԹԵԱՆ ԵՒ ՄԵՐ ՈՐԴԻ ԱՅՍ ԳԱԳԱ[32] ԵՒ ՍՄՊԱՏՍ[33] ԵՒ ԿԵՏԱՅԻ/Ն[34] ԵՒ ԻՄ ՄԵՂԱՅՑ ԹՈՂՈՒԹԵԱՆ ԵՒ ԻՄ ԾՆՈՂԱՅՆ. ԱՐԴ ՈՐ ՀԱԿԱՌԱԿ ԿԱ ԱՅ/Մ ԳՐՈՍ ԿԱՄ ԲԱԳՐԱՏՈՒՆԻ ԿԱՄ ԱԶԱՏ ԿԱՄ ՍԱԼՈՒՔՆ ՆԶՈՎԵԱԼ ԵՂԻՑԻ ՅԱ/ՄԵՆԱԿԱԼԷՆ ԱՅ ԵՒ Ի ՍՈՒՐԲ ԵՐՐ[ՈՐԴՈՒԹԵՆԷՆ] ։ՅԺ։ ՀԱՅՐԱՊԵՏԱՅՆ ԿԱՊԵԱԼ Է /ՊԻՑ Ի ՀՈԳՈՎ ԵՒ ՄԱՐՄՆՈՎ ԵՒ ԲԱԳՐԱՏՈՒՆԻ ԱԶԳԻՍ ՄԵՂԱՅՆ Տ[ԷՐ Է / ՊԻՑԻ ԱՌԱՋԻ ԱՅ. ԻՍԿ ԿԱՏԱՐԻՉՔ ՀՐԱՄԱՆԱՑ ԻՄՈՑ ԱԻՀՆԵԱԼ ԵՂ/[ԻՑԻՆ։] ԵՍ ԳՐԵՑԻ ՄԱԹԵՈՍ ՍԻԱՅՆԱԿԵՑՅ ՏԱՐ /ԱԻՆԵՑԻՍ[35]:

Նկատողություն

Արձանագրության թվականը կարդացվում է ՆՀԲ (1029), որը չի համապատասխանում արձանագրության բովանդակությանը՝ Խոսրովանույշի ժամանակին: Անգամ, եթե Հ-ի փոխարեն կարդալու լինենք Լ (939 թ.)՝ դարձյալ շատ է, հավանաբար Հ-ն գրված է սխալմամբ, փոխանակ Ժ-ի, որ կլինի՝ 963[36]:
7-րդ տող. գրված է ՄԱՐՄՈՎ, փոխանակ ՄԱՐՄՆՈՎ.
9-րդ տող. ՍԻԱՅՆԿԱԵՑՅ, փոխանակ՝ ՍԻԱՅՆԱԿԵՑՅ.
5-րդ տող. ԳՐՈՍ, փոխանակ՝ ԳՐՈՅՍ (Աշխ.Ք):

---

[29] Այս քարը հետագայում տեղափոխվել է և այսօր գտնվում է Վանստանից մոտ 10 կմ հարավ-արևմուտք՝ Գյոյլույսոր գյուղի գերեզմանոցում:

[30] Հայոց թագուհի, իր ամուսնու՝ Աշոտ Գ Ողորմած թագավորի հետ լայն շինարարական գործունեություն է ծավալել: Հիմնադրել են հռչակավոր Սանահնի վանքը՝ 966 թ.:

[31] Շարիաթ-ավատատեր հողատիրոջ օգտին վճարվող տուրք, որ գանձվում էր բնամթերքով, բերքի կամ եկամտի 1/10-րդի չափով (Հայ ժողովրդի պատմություն, հտ 3, Երևան, 1976, էջ 258-259):

[32] Գագիկ Ա Հայոց Բագրատունի թագավոր (990-1020 թթ.):

[33] Սմբատ Բ Տիեզերական Հայոց Բագրատունի թագավոր (977-990 թթ.):

[34] Աշոտ Գ Ողորմած թագավորը և Խոսրովանույշ թագուհին, համաձայն սկզբնաղբյուրների վկայության՝ ունեցել են երեք արու զավակ՝ Սմբատ, Գագիկ, Գուրգեն: Վերջինս դարձել է Տաշիր-Ձորագետի թագավորության հիմնադիրը՝ Կյուրիկե Ա (Գուրգենի փաղաքշական ձև) անունով: Կետա անձնանունը նման է հայոց մեջ ընդունված Կատրա Կատրանիդե իգական անվանը: Ունեցե՞լ են այս անունով դուստր Աշոտ թագավորը և Խոսրովանույշ թագուհին, սկզբնաղբյուրներից հայտնի չէ: Սակայն անհավանական չէ, որ Կետան լիներ մանուկ կամ պատանի Գուրգենի անկան փաղաքշական կամ սովոր ձևը, կամ նույնիսկ գրչի շփոթ:

[35] Արձանագրությունը փորագրող գրչի անունն է: Նրա անվան հիշատակմամբ սկզբնաղբյուրներում այլ վկայություններ հայտնի չեն: Մաթեոս Տարոնացին հայ իրականության մեջ հայտնի ամենավաղ վիմագրիչներից է:

[36] Այս արձանագրության Աշխ.Քալանթարի վերծանությունը, այնտեղ հիշված մի տերմինի (ՍԱԼՈՒՔ) բնույթի կապակցությամբ, հրատարակել է Ս.Ավագյանը (Վիմական արձանագրությունների բառաքննություն, էջ 283-287): Ավագյանի համաձայն հաշվելով պատմական փաստերը, հիշատակված անձանց գործունեության ժամանակը՝ վիմագրի թվականը, վերծանումն է ՀԱՅՈՑ ԵՒ Ը (959 թ.):

5. NEW INSCRIPTIONS FROM VANSTAN (H. Melkonyan and G. Sarkissian)

During the preparatory work for the publication of Ashkharbek Kalantar's manuscript, the editors visited the monument. As mentioned above, two-thirds of the inscriptions described by Kalantar were missing from the site, but several inscriptions absent from the manuscript were found. In view of the importance of the complete publication of the Vanstan inscriptions and the interest shown by Kalantar himself, we present the new findings below, continuing Kalantar's numeration.

68. On the northern wall of St. Virgin church, below the crosses, the following two lines:

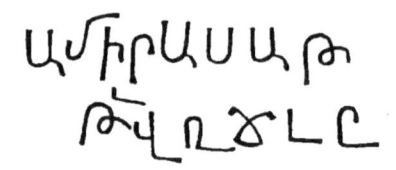

ԱՄԻՐԱՍԱԹ
ԹՎ ՌՁԼԲ

69. Near the previous one, below three other crosses:

: ԹՎ : Լ :

Pl. 12:1

5. Նորահայտ արձանագրություններ Վանստանից (Հ. Մելքոնյան - Գ. Սարգսյան)

1996 թ., Աշխարհբեկ Քալանթարի աշխատանքը հրատարակության պատրաստելու կապակցությամբ, հուշարձանում և շրջակայքում գիրքը կազմողներին հաջողվեց հայտնաբերել մի քանի արձանագրություններ, որոնք տեղ չէին գտել ձեռագրում։

Նկատի ունենալով Վանստանի արձանագրությունների ամբողջական հրապարակման անհրաժեշտությունը, որի՛ շահագրգռություն ցուցաբերել է հենց ինքը՝ Աշխ. Քալանթարը, ստորև ներկայացնում ենք այդ նորահայտ արձանագրությունները, շարունակելով համարակալումը։

68. *Ս.Աստվածածին եկեղեցու* հյուսիսային հիմնապատի վրա, խաչանշանների ներքևում, 2 տող.

ԱՄԻՐԱՍԱԹ ԹՎԻՆ] ՌՃԼԸ (1689 թ.)։

69. Նախորդի մոտ, *երեք այլ խաչանշանների տակ*

ԹՎԻՆ ։Ջ։ (1451թ.)։

70. Near the previous one, below three other crosses:

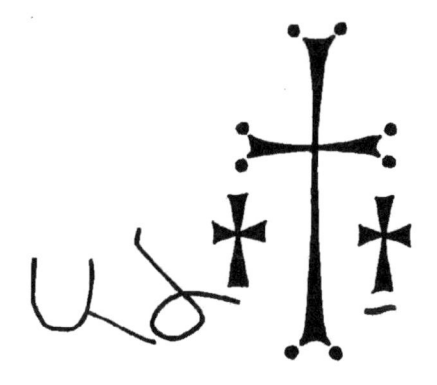

Pl. 12:2

71. Khachkar 20 m north-west of the St. Virgin church, on both sides of the cross, seven lines:[37]

Pl. 12:3

---

[37] The khachkar is engraved on the reverse side of one of the stones of the drum. This remarkable fact indicates that the church was destroyed already in 1597.

NEW INSCRIPTIONS FROM VANSTAN

70. Նախորդի մոտ, երեք այլ խաչանշանների տակ.

ԱԾ (Աստված):

71. *Խաչքար*, Ս.Աստվածածին եկեղեցուց շուրջ 20 մ հարավ-արևմուտք, քիվին և խաչանշանի երկու կողմերում, 7 տող[37].

ՄԲ ԽԱՁՍ ԲԱ[ՐԵ]ԽԱԻՍ ՍԱՐԳԻ[Ս]ԻՆ, ՈՐ
... ...ՂԱՁ ... / ԱՏ / ԱՇ / ԽԱ / ՏԵՑԻ
ԽՈՐ .../ ԹՎԻՆ] ՌԽՁ (1597 թ.):

---

[37] Խաչքարը քանդակված է եկեղեցու քթուկի նիստավոր քիվի քարերից մեկի վրա, հակառակ երեսին։ Այս խաչքարի առկայությունը ուշագրավ է, քանի որ փաստում է արդեն 1597թ. եկեղեցու ավերված լինելու հանգամանքը։

72. Khachkar 10 m south-west of the St. Virgin church, found in the ruins, 3 lines on its lower part:[38]

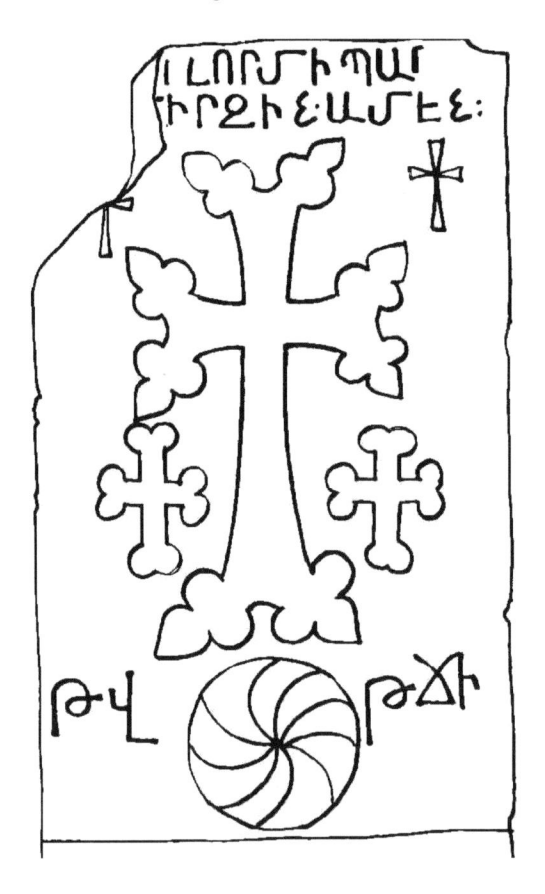

Pl. 13:1

73. Fragment of a khachkar, about 100 m south-west of the St. Virgin church, in the ruins. On its lower part:

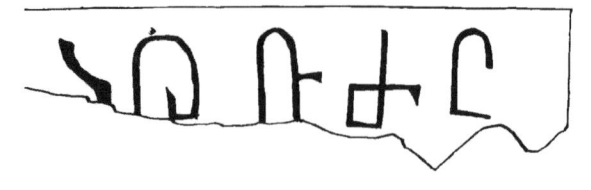

Pl. 13:2

---

[38] One can assume that the khachkar is dedicated to Amirze, mentioned in No. 47.

72. *Խաչքար*, Ս.Աստվածածին եկեղեցուց շուրջ 10 մ հարավ-արևմուտք, փլատակների մեջ, քիվին և ստորին մասում, 3 տող[38].

⌈ՔՍ ԱԾ ՈՂՈՐՄԻ ՊԱՐ⌈ՈՆ⌉/...⌈Ա⌉ՆԻՐՉԻՆ

ԱՄԷՆ: / ԹՎԻՆ ՋԺԻ (1471թ.):

73. *Խաչքարի բեկոր*, Ս.Աստվածածին եկեղեցուց շուրջ 100 մ հարավ-արևմուտք, փլատակների մեջ, ստորին մասում.

ԹՎԻՆ ՌԺԸ (1569թ.):

---

[38] Կարծում ենք, որ խաչքարը նվիրված է թիվ 47 արձանագրության մեջ որպես պատվիրատու վկայված Ամիրզեին:

74. Four-sided base of a pillar found 30 m north of the church. Two lines on one of the faces:[39]

Pl. 14:1

75. Grave-stone to the north-east of the St. Virgin church, on a steep slope. Five lines:

Pl. 14:3

---

[39] An eagle is engraved on the second facet and an arch on the third.

74. *Սյան քառակող խարսխաքար*[39] եկեղեցուց հյուսիս մոտ 30 մ, փլատակների մեջ։ Նիստին, 2 տող.

ԹՎԻՆյ ՈԻԱ (1572 թ.):

75. *Արձանագրված շինաքար*, Ս.Աստվածածին եկեղեցու հյուսիս-արևելյան կողմում, թեք լանջին, 5 տող.

ԿԱՄԱԻ ԱՅ .... / .... ԱՅ
...Մ.Բ... / ..Հ ԵԻ ՍՊԱՍԱԻՈՐՔ ... /
ԻՆ... / ԵՆ ԿԱՄ ....:

---

[39] Խարսխաքարի նիստերից մեկին քառատարած արծվի քանդակ է, մյուսին՝ զույգ սյուներով կամարի ռելյեֆ պատկեր:

76. Grave-stone found 10 m from the church. A few lines above the crosses:

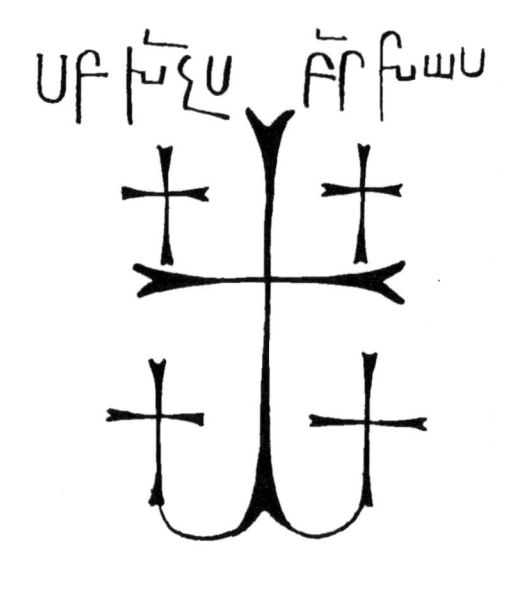

ՍՐ ԽՀՍ ՔՐ ԽԱՍ

Pl. 14:2

76. *Արձանագրված շինքար*, Ս.Աստվածածին եկեղեցուց 10 մ արևմուտք, խաչանշանների վերևում, 1 տող:

ՍԲ ԽԱՉՍ ԲԱՐԵԽԱԻՍ...:

KALANTAR'S STUDIES ON EPIGRAPHY

by H. MELKONYAN and G. SARKISSIAN

Epigraphy as a scientific discipline developed in Europe in the XIVth-XVth centuries, when the great value of inscriptions as historical sources was realised. During that period several scholars travelled through countries possessing ancient cultural monuments and copied the inscriptions carved on stones and various architectural monuments that contained original information on the history of human civilization from its very early epochs.

The development of historiography required the development of scientific principles of copying, deciphering, collection and publication of epigraphic data. This activity was shaped in the XIXth century.

Containing ancient history and literature, inscriptions were an essential part of the material culture in Armenia. Already in the Vth century, Armenian historians were using sources on the various languages that survived in Armenia. Movses Khorenatzi in particular quoted inscriptions in Greek and Aramaic in his Vth-century "Armenian History."

In the XIIIth century, Stephanos Orbelian, the metropolitan of the Syunik state of Armenia, did essential work in gathering and using numerous inscriptions in his historical work. In the XVIIth century, Zakaria Sarkavag Kanakertzi published dozens of inscriptions carved on the walls of the Hovhanavank church in the third volume of his "History."

The systematic collection and publication of inscriptions found in Armenia started in the early XIXth century, when Minas Bzhishkyantz (1830), archbishop Hovhannes Shahkhatunyantz (1842) and Sargis Jalaliantz (1842-1853) published several hundred of them. Remarkable studies were also published in the second half of the XIXth century, including those of Nerses Sargissian, Abel Mkhitarian, Garegin Srvandztian, physician Gabriel Hovhannisian (Kajberuni), Makar Barkhudariantz, and archbishop Mesrop Smbatiantz. Finally, the "Annual Review of Inscriptions" of Karapet Kostaniantz appeared in 1913, which was aimed at the scientific circulation of materials on Armenian inscriptions.

In 1879, the Russian Archaeological Assembly outlined the importance of the collection and publication of cuneiform, Armenian, Georgian and Hebrew inscriptions found in the Caucasian area. Therefore Mkrtich Emin, in a volume published in 1881 in Moscow, included the inscriptions of Kars, Ani and their vicinities, in both Armenian and parallel Russian translations.

The search, publication and study of Armenian inscriptions using modern scientific concepts is associated with the name of Nicholas Marr, head of the renowned excavations of the mediaeval Armenian capital, Ani. Marr, together with his student Iosef Orbeli, gathered and studied numerous inscriptions uncovered during the excavations of Ani. Later Orbeli prepared the Corpus (Survey) of Ani Inscriptions.[1]

---

[1] *Corpus of Armenian Inscriptions*, Erevan, 1965.

Ashkharbek Kalantar grew up in this creative atmosphere, as an active participant in the archaeological campaigns at Ani (supervisor in 1914), and as a student of Marr, Turaev, Smirnov, Bartold and other outstanding scholars. Thus, it was not by accident that in addition to Kalantar's achievements in various areas of Caucasian and Armenian history, he also made important contributions in epigraphy.

Kalantar began his participation in the Ani expeditions in 1907 while he was still a student in the division of Armenian-Georgian Philology in the Faculty of Oriental Linguistics of St. Petersburg University. That same year he published his first article on the Ani excavations.[2] The following episode of this early period, which is described by Orbeli, illustrates young Kalantar's proficiency in epigraphy. At Ani, in 1906, during excavations in the area near the church of St. Grigor Lusavorich (the Illuminator), which was built in 1001-1015 by king Gagik I Bagratuni (990-1020), the famous statue of the king Gagik holding a model of the church was discovered. At the same time, 131 fragments of a large inscription were found, which enabled Marr to begin the difficult work of its reconstruction. Due to a lack of time, Marr succeeded in reading only the two last lines. The rest were read with high proficiency by young Ashkharbek Kalantar.[3] His reading is included by Orbeli in the Corpus of Ani inscriptions.

However, the Kalantar's own serious epigraphical studies started in 1912, when the Imperial Russian Academy sent him to the Caucasus, to the Erevan state, to collect and study the Armenian inscriptions of Imirzek and its vicinity. This was at Marr's instigation, who had recognised the importance of this remarkable monument and of its inscriptions during his previous trips in Armenia. He decided to involve his best student in this work.

On July 12, 1912, upon "getting the necessary instructions" (from Marr), Kalantar left Ani for Imirzek. On the way, he investigated the pagan temple in Garni, the Christian monuments of the village and the Havutz Tar and Aghjotz Surb Stephanos monasteries — mediaeval Armenian religious centres. He also studied the Vth-century basilica in Bayburt.

In just three weeks in Imirzek, with the help of two experienced workers (brought from Ani) and several inhabitants of the village, he opened the ruins of the St. Virgin church, its gavith (pre-entrance) and the vicinity (Pl. 15 and 16). They discovered numerous inscriptions, cross-stones (khachkars), grave-stones, etc. Kalantar succeeded in copying over 60 inscriptions. He reported the preliminary results of this trip at the session of the Imperial Academy held on January 16, 1913, and he published a brief article (in Russian) in the Bulletin of the Academy.[4] Later, Kalantar also prepared two detailed manuscripts on the inscriptions of Imirzek, both of which unfortunately remained unpublished. The materials of the first one were damaged in the publishing house of the Academy during the 1924 flood in St. Petersburg. The recovered (second) manuscript survived by chance in the archive of the Institute of Archaeology and Ethnography in Erevan, after the arrest of Kalantar in early 1938 by the Stalin regime. We present this work herein, both in Armenian and English, along with detailed reconstructions of the inscriptions, their copies and photos.

The investigations conducted by ourselves at the site in 1996-1997 showed that the author, being familiar with the tiny peculiarities of mediaeval Armenian language (grabar), had perfectly read the inscriptions and restored the missing and damaged parts with great accuracy. Understanding the

---

[2] A. Kalantar, Excavations in Ani, *Horizon*, July 1907.
[3] I.A. Orbeli, *Selected Papers*, Erevan, 1963, p. 41. *Corpus of Armenian Inscriptions*, Erevan, 1965.
[4] A. Loris-Kalantar, Preliminary Report on the Trip to Imirzek in the Summer of 1912, *Bull. Acad. Impériale des Sciences de St.-Pétersbourg*, Série VI, 1913.

exceptional importance of exact copies of the inscriptions, he had prepared them with extreme care, along with the photos. The exact depiction of the palaeography is crucial for archaeological purposes, and occasionally it can also allow the inscriptions to be dated.

The inscriptions of Imirzek have exceptional historical importance. This religious centre is rarely mentioned in historical chronicles, so that the inscriptions are occasionally the only source for the study of a number of events of the XIII-XVIth centuries. Particularly, the inscriptions reveal the original name of the monastery, Vanstan, the date of its foundation, the name of its builder, the names of the key figures of the monastery, its benefactors and the names of geographical sites in its vicinity.

The majority of the inscriptions discovered and read by Kalantar in 1912 do not survive today, and therefore the data in his manuscript now have the value of originals.[5]

The years 1912 and 1913 were rather fruitful ones for Kalantar. At the behest of the Ethnographic Division of the Russian Museum of Alexander III (see p. XVII above) he was sent to the Lori, Nakhijevan and Surmalu districts (the latter two now in Turkey) of Erevan state, to study the religion, life and habits of the Kurd-Ezides. At the same time he studied the ancient architectural monuments of the region, in particular the Vth-VIth century basilica of Zor and the XIIIth-century caravanserai.[6]

On the inner side of the north-east wall of the basilica he discovered a damaged Armenian inscription, which he attributed to a later epoch, one that was no earlier than the Xth-XIth centuries. He therefore disagreed with the conclusions of Alishan, who identified Zor with the Kamrjadzor monastery. Kalantar cited the Armenian historian of the Xth-XIth centuries, Stephanos Taronatzi (Asoghik), who stated that Kamrjadzor was founded in the Xth century in the Arshakuni state. While studying the caravanserai, he discovered an Arabic inscription on the frame of its window: "Ashot, the Builder." In comparing the caravanserai with the bas-reliefs of the prince's palace in Ani and the sculptures near the entrance of its St. Arakelotz (Apostles) church, he was able to identify the sculpture under the upper arch of caravanserai with a similar sculpture in Vanstan. On this basis, he attributed the caravanserai to the XIIIth century.

In the summer of 1913, Kalantar was sent by the Imperial Russian Academy to the Lori region in Armenia. There he studied the basilica in Odzun (VIth cent.), the monuments in Horomayr (XIIth-XIIIth cent.), Kobayr (XIIth-XIIIth cent.) and the St. Grigor monastery (XIIth-XIIIth cent.) in Dsegh. He reported the results of the trip on September 13, 1913, at the session of the Historical-Philological Division of the Academy. As he noted in his lecture, the great quantity of the inscriptions and the shortage of photographic materials prevented the complete survey and copying of the inscriptions of the region, although he did succeed in completing the inscriptions of Odzun and Kobayr. In total, he copied over 120 inscriptions, of which only four or five had been previously published. Particularly interesting were his conclusions concerning the epigraphic and dialectal characteristics of the Lori region, which differed from those of other regions of Armenia in the unusual and complicated use of brackets.

During those years Kalantar continued to be very actively involved in the archaeological expeditions to Ani. By that time his works and publications had made of him an authority.

---

[5] Part of the original negatives are kept in the archive of the Museum of History, Erevan.
[6] A. Loris-Kalantar, The Basilica in Zor and the Ruins of an Ancient Caravanserai, *Khristiansky Vostok* III, 101, 1914; English translation in: A. Kalantar, *Armenia: From the Stone Age to the Middle Ages. Selected Papers* (Ed. by G. Karakhanian), *Civilisations du Proche Orient*, Série 1, vol. 2, Neuchâtel, Paris, 1994.

Therefore, on March 15, 1914, he was elected as a member-employee of the Imperial Archaeological Society in St. Petersburg; and that same year he was also appointed to head the thirteenth archaeological campaign to Ani while (see p. XIX above) Marr was engaged in linguistic studies in Daghestan. A unique document dated May 22, 1914, was issued to him by the Imperial Archaeological Society, the so-called "Open List," (see p. XVIII above) granting him permission "to perform archaeological excavations in the city of Ani of Kars state and its environs" and also guaranteeing him the support of all civil and military officials.

In 1917, the Imperial Archaeological Society organized the second Van expedition with the participation of Nicholas Adontz and Kalantar. According to one document, Kalantar had "to undertake systematic studies of the monuments of the Van district and area occupied by the Russian army," perform excavations and collect inscriptions in Van, Haykaberd etc. Among other achievements, they succeeded in finding over 50 new cuneiform inscriptions in the vicinity of Van.

Kalantar's epigraphical work was not limited to Armenian inscriptions. He also copied, collected and read a number of Urartian inscriptions.[7] His collection of glass-plates of Urartian inscriptions was well known among experts, being cited by, among others, Meshchaninov, Lehmann-Haupt, Belck, Friedrich, Basmajian, and Reinach. Unfortunately, this unique collection (in several huge boxes) was confiscated from Kalantar's home during his arrest, and its whereabouts are still unknown.

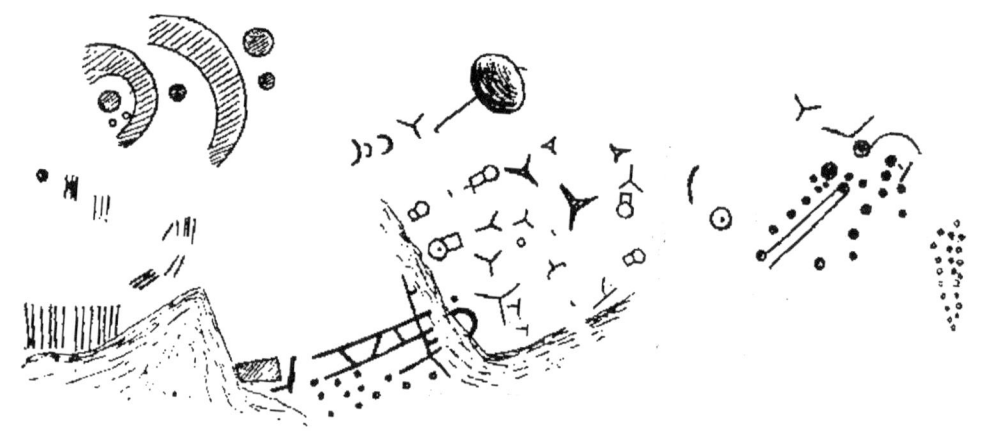

The 'Armavir Inscription' (see also Pl. 24 : 2). From *Revue Archéologique* 30 (1929), 43.

In 1929, Kalantar published a unique article on previously unknown hieroglyphs that had been discovered on the Armavir hill in Armenia.[8] The Armavir stone that bore those inscriptions has unfortunately not survived. Although the problem has been revisited numerous times since 1929, the precise meaning of the hieroglyphs remains unclear. They presumably belong to the same epoch as the rock-carved figures that have been discovered elsewhere in Armenia.

---

[7] A. Kalantar, Two Cuneiform Inscriptions of Rusa, Son of Sardur, *Bull. Comm. Ancient Monum* 3, p. 1, 1927; A Newly Found Chaldean Inscription from the Village of Janfida, *Bull. Comm. Ancient Monum.* 4, p. 1, 1930; English translation in : A. Kalantar, *Armenia : From the Stone Age...*, op. cit. n. 6 above.

[8] A. Kalantar, Inscriptions d'Arménie en caractères inconnus, *Revue Archéologique* 30, 1929.

While analysing the phenomenon of cult of water existing in Armenia in prehistoric times, he discovered a pre-Urartian irrigation system on the slopes of Mt. Aragatz and Geghama range,[9] and he is quoting numerous mediaeval inscriptions containing reflections on that phenomenon of the remote past.

In 1917, due to the wartime conditions, the Ani expeditions were cancelled, leaving a rich archaeological collection on the site. Therefore, in 1918, in accordance with a resolution of the Chair of the Armenian National Assembly (see p. XX above), Kalantar, with the help of 17 young people, organized the evacuation from Ani of 27 boxes containing over 14000 archaeological objects, which are currently housed in the Museum of History in Erevan.

In 1920, conditions allowed a brief resumption of investigations at Ani. Kalantar used this opportunity to study the mediaeval monuments in Ani, Tekor and in their vicinities. In August and September of 1920, he undertook a trip to study the monuments in Tekor, Khtzkonk, Arjo-Arij, Agarak, Jalal, Tzpni, Nakhjevan, Bagaran and Mren (all now in Turkey). He recorded detailed descriptions of these monuments and sketched copies of 29 inscriptions, of which only six had been published previously. Some of them remain the only copies of inscriptions which are now lost. This notebook was first published in English in 1994.[10]

Kalantar's epigraphic activity increased while he served as the Scientific Secretary of the Commission of Ancient Monuments of Armenia, beginning with its foundation in 1923. (In 1919, he had been named head of the Division of Ancient Monuments in the Ministry of Culture.) The Commission was chaired by architect Academician Alexander Tamanian and comprised distinguished Armenian intellectuals, including painter Martiros Sarian, architect Toros Toramanian, ethnographer Ervand Shahaziz, art historian Garegin Levonian, ethnographer Stephan Lisitzian, architect Taragros and others.

From that time on, during some 15 fruitful years, Kalantar organized over 30 expeditions to various regions of Armenia, surveys, excavations etc. His pedagogical activity was no less impressive : he was one of the seven founding members of Erevan University, the founder of its Chair of Archaeology, the author of the first textbook on archaeology in Armenian, and up to the end of his life he was Professor of the University, raising generations of scholars.[11]

To conclude this brief essay on Kalantar's work in epigraphy, we mention a report from Marr of 1925, wherein his remarkable success at Ani is highlighted, both in terms of the scientific organization of excavations and in the study of the inscriptions. Marr wrote : "He (Kalantar) is one of the most reliable specialists in the reading of inscriptions, and the only one upon whom one can rely in Armenian epigraphy. Kalantar is a historian of material culture who utilizes Armenian literary monuments, especially epigraphic ones. It is enough to mention that among the newly discovered monuments, some 3000 are Armenian inscriptions."

The publication of "The Inscriptions of Vanstan" in the present volume, apart from having unique scientific value, is also a memorial to Ashkharbek Kalantar.

---

[9] A. Kalantar, An Ancient Irrigation System in Armenia, *Bulletin of Inst. of History and Literature* 3, Erevan, p. 171, 1937 ; English translation in : A. Kalantar, *Armenia : From the Stone Age...*, *op. cit.* n. 6 above.

[10] A. Kalantar, *Armenia : From the Stone Age...*, *op. cit.* n. 6 above.

[11] For additional details on Kalantar's life and work, see the biographical essay by G. Karakhanian in : A. Kalantar, *Armenia : From the Stone Age...*, *op. cit.* n. 6 above.

VANSTAN IN THE HISTORICAL CHRONICLES

by H. MELKONYAN and G. SARKISSIAN

The Vanstan monastery was one of the religious and cultural centres of mediaeval Armenia. At present, its ruins are located in the Khosrov National Reservation, on the right bank of the Asat River, 15 km south-west of Garni, near the abandoned village of Imirzek. The ruins, which are comprised of the lower portions of the walls of the St. Virgin church and parts of the necropolis, are the remains of the once famous monastery of the Vostan district of the Ayrarat state of mediaeval Armenia. At that time it was situated on the road from Syunik state (via the town of Urtz) to Geghard, Garni, Dvin and Vagharshapat. Even today the remains of this road are visible in the vicinity of Vanstan, Geghard, Havutz Tar etc. (see the map), including the ruined mediaeval bridge (Pl. 24 : 1).

The St. Virgin church is situated on a rock, which is rather steep in the south-east direction. This circumstance forced the builder to construct first a horizontal basalt area with complicated basement (Pl. 18). The space exactly below the main altar, with an area of about 2.4 x 2.5 m and a depth of 1.5 m, was probably used as a hiding place for the valuables of the monastery (Pl. 17 and 19). The basement of the church is situated on an extra horizontal stone row.

The plan of the church represents a dome-covered hall — a style popular in mediaeval Armenia. The external dimensions of the church are 12 x 9 m. It is oriented from east to west, with a 4 : 3 ratio of the quadrangle sides (Pl. 17). This ratio was widely used in a number of churches of that period, including Cathoghike of Geghard, St. Sion of Saghmosavank, St. Harutyun of Harij, St. Grigor of Goshavank etc. Most of the processed stones of the church bear the marks of the workers. The only entrance is from the west. All its facades, except the western one, had traditional cavities of triangular cross section, the inner quadrangular hall ending by the altar on the east. A broadening of the dome-covered hall via the narrowing of the naves can be observed.

The western wall-pillars of the rounded part of the hall touched the western altar wall. These pillars stood on bases situated 1.3 m from the walls. The drum of the church was multi-sided.

Judging from the fragments which have survived, the St. Virgin church had a rich decor. This is apparent in the front of the stage, the triangular cavities and frames of the windows, the pre-entrance, the sculptures of the facets of the drum and numerous other tiny reliefs.

The Vanstan monastery began attracting the attention of historians long ago. Ghevond Alishan, while speaking about the monuments of the Mazaz district of Ayrarat state, mentioned the "Imirzek or Mirzik ancient ruined church."[1] Alishan was not aware of the original name of the church of Vanstan. On another occasion he cited the manuscript of Simeon Erevantzi, wherein the name Vanstan is mentioned, without recognizing the identity of these monuments.

---

[1] G. Alishan, *Ayrarat*, Venice, 1890, p. 360 (in Armenian).

In 1907-1908, the expedition of the Moscow Imperial Archaeological Society had studied and published numerous materials on Armenian mediaeval architecture. The data collected by V. Sisoev and Taragros were published in 1913 under the editorship of Kuchuk-Hovhannesian. Among other materials, the monuments of the Kegha canyon are mentioned, including the plan of the St. Virgin church of Vanstan, a few photos and four inscriptions.[2] Under its original name, the Vanstan church was first mentioned by Garegin Hovsepian, who also entertained some questions about its history.[3] The Vanstan church was also mentioned on various occasions by I. Orbeli and N. Tokarsky,[4] and several inscriptions of Vanstan were discussed by S. Avagian as well.[5] Finally, one of the sculptures found in Vanstan during Kalantar's excavations is discussed by P. Donabedian.[6]

Ashkharbek Kalantar, who initiated the scientific investigation of the Vanstan monastery, organized the excavations of the monument in 1912, at which time he also opened the ruins of the St. Virgin church and discovered numerous inscriptions and unique architectural fragments. He published two preliminary reports on the excavations.[7] He discovered over sixty inscriptions on the walls of the church and on grave-stones. These inscriptions have enabled us to reconstruct the various aspects of life within the monastery, the names of its inhabitants, etc. Just as an example, the inscriptions surrounding the entrance (No. 1)[8] inform us that the founder and first religious head of the monastery was David.[9]

The historical value of inscription No. 2 is exceptional. First, it informs us of the exact date of the foundation of the church by Ter David. Second, Ter David is said to have been also the head of Khor Virap monastery, the religious centre of Ayrarat state, where he built the Katoghike church of Khor Virap and its surrounding wall. It is important to note that this is the oldest known mention of building activities in Khor Virap.

The inscription enables us to reconstruct the date of the building activities in both Khor Virap and Vanstan, because both are attributed to "the time of Ivane," and we know that this Ivane (Zakarian) ruled from 1212 to 1227.[10] The circumstances of the foundation of Vanstan monastery are also quite remarkable, inasmuch as it was built to house the Hatzunyatz St. Nshan.[11] The renowned political and military historian Shapuh Bagratuni tells us that the Byzantine emperor Herakl, upon returning from a military campaign, presented a relic piece of the cross of Jesus Christ to the princess

---

[2] *Materials on the Archaeology of the Caucasus* XIII, Moscow, 1913, p. 67-69.

[3] G. Hovsepian, *Khotakeratz St. Nshan, an Example of Armenian Gold-Art of the XIIIth Century*, Tiflis, 1912, p. 3 ; id., *Khaghbakiank or Proshiank in Armenian History*, Vagharshapat, 1928, p. 66, 80, 250.

[4] I. Orbeli, *The Armenian Monuments of Akhtamar Island. Selected Papers*, vol. 1, Moscow, 1968, p. 118 ; N. Tokarsky, *Armenian Architecture in the IVth-XIVth Centuries*, Erevan, 1961, p. 338.

[5] S. Avagian, *Analysis of Stone-Inscriptions*, Erevan, p. 272, 283-287, and 340-342.

[6] P. Donabedian, On the Bas-Relief of the Vanstan Church, *Historical-Philological Journal* 1, Erevan, 1979, p. 154-165.

[7] A. Loris-Kalantar, On the Trip to Erevan State, *Comm. of the Oriental Branch of the Imperial Archaeological Society* XXII, St. Petersburg, 1914, p. IX-X ; id., Preliminary Report on the Trip to Imirzek in 1912, *Bull. Acad. Impériale des Sciences de St.-Pétersbourg*, 1913.

[8] The numbers are given in accordance with Kalantar's numeration.

[9] No biographical details about Ter David are known. His relatives, including his father (Grigor), his mother (Aghut), his grandfather (Hasamatin) and one of his brothers (Khalt), are mentioned in the same inscription. David is also mentioned in inscriptions Nos. 3, 4 and 5.

[10] *History of the Armenian Nation* 3, Erevan, 1976, p. 976.

[11] A. Sahakian, The History of the Hatzunyatz Cross, *Historical Philological Journal* 4, Erevan, 1981, p. 153 ; id., The Pseudo-History of the Hatzunyatz Cross and its Oral Versions, *Historical Philological Journal* 3, 1982, p. 135.

of Syunik, Byuregh, and that this relic later became known as Hatzunyatz St. Nshan, named as the village of Hatzyun in the Artaz district of Vaspurakan state.[12]

In this same Artaz district, the princess of Syunik founded a monastery, where the holy relic was kept.[13] Some later chronicles associate this relic with the Arkaz St. Khach (Cross) church of Syunik, and Khachkavank in Karin.[14] Esayi Nchetzi, the rector of the renowned mediaeval Armenian University of Gladzor, in his book of 1284, mentions the three most sacred relics kept in Armenia. The first was the Hatzunyatz St. Nshan, and the other two were the Khor Virap and the Ark of Noah (on Mt. Ararat).[15] It is possible that Stephanos Orbelian, the 'metropolitan' of Syunik, was well aware that the relic of the holy cross was kept not in Syunik, but in Vanstan. It is not clear, however, why the Vanstan monastery was called St. Virgin and not, say, after the Hatzunyatz St. Nshan relic.

Upon founding Vanstan, Ter David presented a number of gifts to the monastery. The inscriptions describe its flourishing life, due to a number of benefactors, estates, etc, especially in the second half of the XIIIth century, when it was under the supervision of Grigor. The inscriptions inform us that both Grigor and his brother Vardan, were students of the famous scholar, archbishop Grigor Bjnetzi, the religious head of Ayrarat state. Inscriptions No. 8-10 also mention Grigor, as the head of the Khor Virap and Vanstan monasteries in the seventh and eighth decades of the XIIIth century. Grigor, with his brother Vardan,[16] participated in a religious meeting held in Dzagavan in 1270, where several important resolutions were adopted to regulate religious and civil interactions in the country. The activities of Grigor and Vardan are mainly associated with Khor Virap, where both were buried.

In 1283, Grigor covered the floor of the church with stone, at which time he presented a number of gifts to the monastery. At the time of Grigor, the benefactor of the monastery was the political and military figure Sadun Artzruni, one of the organizers of the Dzagavan meeting. He was one of the powerful princes of Northern Armenia, the amira of Tiflis, the owner of Mahkanaberd and Kayen, and he is mentioned in the Vanstan inscriptions twice (1278, 1283) as "atapak and amirspasalar." According to the first inscription, Sadun presented two mills and an estate to Vanstan, and according to the other, he gave twenty dahekans (golden coins). From these inscriptions one can conclude that Vanstan was part of Sadun's estate. However, Garegin Hovsepian (*op. cit.*, n. 13) attributed Vanstan to the Proshian prince dynasty, and according to the historian Hovhanness Draskhanakertzi, the Keghi Berd (fortress), which was situated in the vicinity of Vanstan, belonged to the Bagratunies in the IXth-Xth centuries.[17] The latter fact is indirectly supported by an inscription of 959, which was discovered by Kalantar in Kyopri-Kulakh,[18] stating that the wife of Ashot Bagratuni, the queen Khosrovanuysh, had cancelled certain taxes (shariat) from a village.

---

[12] H. Ajarian, *Handbook of Armenian Names* 1, Erevan, 1942, p. 146 ; G. Alishan, *Sisakan, Chronicle of Syunik*, Venice, 1893, p. 14 ; N. Adontz, *Armenia in the Epoch of Justinian*, 1908, St. Petersburg, p. 131 ; S. Eremian, *Armenia by 'Ashkharatzuytz'*, Erevan, 1963, p. 62.

[13] *History of Shapuh Bagratuni*, Echmiadzin, 1921, p. 14.

[14] A. Sahakian, *op. cit.* n. 11 above, p. 136.

[15] *Comments on Armenian Manuscripts of the XIIIth Century*, Erevan, 1984, p. 556, 557.

[16] Vardan Areveltzi was another renowned mediaeval Armenian scholar and historian who left a rich scientific heritage ; see H. Ajarian, *Handbook of Armenian Names* 5, Erevan, 1962, p. 87.

[17] *History* by Catholicos Hovhannes Draskhanakertzi, Tiflis, 1912, p. 356.

[18] The exact date of the inscription was uncovered by S. Avagian, *op. cit.* n. 5 above, p. 284.

In the late XIIth and early XIIIth centuries, after a joint Armenian-Georgian army had freed Armenia from the Seljuks, this region passed to Ivane Zakarian, who had ordered David to found the monastery. In 1225, in a battle near Garni, the Armenian-Georgian army was defeated by Jalal-ad-Din, the son of Khorezmshah, and Ivane escaped to Keghi fortress along with a small group of compatriots.[19]

One of the Vanstan inscriptions (No. 11), which was written on behalf of the owners of Keghi Berd and dated to the seventh and eighth decades of the XIIIth century, describes the gifts donated to the monastery by them. Although there is no direct evidence concerning the identity of the owners of the Keghi Berd and its environs, according to Garegin Hovsepian, the inscriptions in Geghard and on the khachkar of 1233 found in the nearby village of Gilanlar,[20] attribute these areas to Khaghbakian or the Proshian princes.[21] In particular, he identified the "Tajer" of the Vanstan inscription No. 59 with the princess Tajer who was the wife of prince Amir-Hasan I Proshian.

However, the inscriptions of Sadun Artzruni discovered in Vanstan indicate that even if this region belonged to the Proshian dynasty in the first half of the XIIIth century, it was under the control of the grand prince of Mahkanaberd during the second half of this century. According to the historical chronicles, it later passed to the Zakarians, and then in the sixth decade of the XIVth century, to the Jelairians and Tamurians.[22] The consequences of the campaign by Tamerlane and his successors in the 1380s were especially hard for Armenia.[23] Step by step Armenia became the arena of active military operations, when numerous towns and villages were ruined, a process described in detail by the historian Tovma Metzopetzi.[24] In the early XVIth century, Armenia was ruled by the Safavid dynasty of Iran, after which a long war raged between Iran and Turkey. Even before, in the early XVth century, the majority of Armenia's once powerful prince dynasties — the Pahlavunies, Vachutians, Orbelians, Proshians and others — were weakened. To save their estates from foreign rulers, they had to donate them to monasteries. Thus monasteries undertook the crucial rule of handling the numerous internal affairs of the country.

The chronicles indicate that the Vanstan monastery flourished and played an important role in the religious and cultural-educational life of the Ayrarat state as late as the XVIth century. Almost half the inscriptions of this period mention benefactors and various gifts, estates, gardens, sheep, cheese etc. Fifteen mention money that had been donated (golden dahekans). Some of the names of the benefactors, such as Gishuk and Sisik in inscription No. 22 (without date), are impossible to identify.

The next mention of Vanstan monastery occurs in connection with 1441, one of the most memorable dates in the history of the Armenian church. 1441 was the year in which the chair of the Armenian patriarch was officially transferred from Sis of Kilikia to Vagharshapat (Echmiadzin). A holy meeting in which over 300 bishops and vartapets participated was first held in Erevan and afterwards in Vagharshapat. After a long debate, Kirakos of Khor Virap was elected catholicos (patriarch).

---

[19] *History of Sisakan State* by Stephanos Orbelian, Archbishop of Syunik, Tiflis, 1910, p. 399.
[20] This khachkar is now in Echmiadzin.
[21] G. Hovsepian, *op. cit.* n. 3 above, p. 62.
[22] L. Babaian, *The Social, Economic and Political History of Armenia in the XIIIth-XIVth Centuries*, Erevan, 1964, p. 352.
[23] Grigor Tzerentz (Khlatetzi), Chronicle of Catastrophes, in : *Comments on XVth-century Armenian Manuscripts* I (Ed. by L. Khachikian), 1955, p. 272.
[24] Tovma Metzopetzi, *The History of Tamerlane and his Successors*, Paris, 1860.

The Vanstan monastery is also mentioned in comments to the Bible recopied in 1460 by Galust in the Aghjotz Surb Stephanos monastery.[25] That manuscript refers to both Surb Stephanos and Vanstan as important monasteries of the region, and mentions as well as two persons (Mirza and Srvanshin) who are also found in Vanstan inscriptions (No. 54 and 49). Vanstan is later mentioned in a manuscript (Mashtotz) recopied in 1560 by Khad for bishop Hayrapet.[26] We believe that the copyist (Khad) was also the author of the inscription on the grave-stone of bishop Khad, discovered in Vanstan (No. 32).

The latest inscription found in Vanstan belongs to the XVIth century,[27] thus indicating the time of the decline of the monastery. Of crucial importance for the dating of the final period of Vanstan monastery is a fragment of the drum of the church discovered in 1997. On the back of this stone, a khachkar of 1597 is engraved, indicating the year when the church had already been destroyed (Pl. 12 : 3, 4).

Thus, the Vanstan monastery had most probably ceased its activity by late XVIth century. This conclusion is indirectly supported by a manuscript dating to 1608 describing the campaign of Abbas, shah of Iran, and its terrible consequences for Armenia. According to this text, most of the atrocities occurred in the caves of Garni canyon and its vicinity.[28] Although the Vanstan church is not mentioned directly in the manuscript in question, some of the nearby mountains are named. The author states that Garni and its vicinity were emptied of their Armenian population. The historian Arakel Davrighetzi also mentions the displacement of the Armenian population, as well as violence, starvation (1606-1609) in Garni and its vicinity, and the subsequent reoccupation by foreign shepherd tribes.[29]

The last mention of Vanstan is attributed to the XVIIIth century. The catholicos Simeon Erevantzi (1763-1780), while speaking about Khor Virap, mentioned Vanstan as one of the villages paying taxes to Khor Virap.[30] It is unclear from this whether the monastery was active or not. It was presumably already ruined before the mighty earthquake of 1769. This conclusion is supported by the absence of any inscriptions dated later than the XVIth century. Thus, the inscriptions of Vanstan add essential color to the XIII-XVIth century history of Armenia and of the region.

---

[25] V. Hakobian, A. Hovhannissian, *Comments on Armenian Manuscripts of the XVIIth Century*, Erevan, 1974, p. 435.
[26] G. Hovsepian, *op. cit.* n. 3 above.
[27] An inscription dated 1689 (No. 69) was carved on the northern wall of the church after its destruction.
[28] V. Hakobian, A. Hovhannissian, *op. cit.* n. 25 above, p. 287.
[29] *The History of Arakel Davrighetzi*, Vagharshapat, 1896, p. 47, 81.
[30] Simeon Erevantzi, *Chronicle (Jambr)*, Vagharshapat, 1873, p. 280.

APPENDICES

I. PRELIMINARY REPORT ON THE TRIP TO IMIRZEK IN THE SUMMER OF 1912 *

The ruins of Imirzek, which are by no means the only ones in the canyon of the river Azat (Garni), attracted the attention of Academician N. Marr due to the abundance of Armenian inscriptions found there. The idea of an urgent epigraphic study of this unknown ancient site was therefore proposed. I had the honor to be the executor of this task.

On July 12, 1912, upon receiving the necessary instructions, I left Ani for Imirzek. While on the way, in the Garni archaeological area, I examined the Garni antiquities uncovered during the excavations of N. Marr, and those located near the Havutz-Tar monastery and the Amenaprkich church. Bypassing then the monastery Surb-Stephanos, staying higher on the road and following along the river Azat (Garni), I discovered a remarkable old, small church in the Turkish settlement of Bayburt — a well preserved basilica, presently used as a shed. In the evening of July 15th, I arrived in Imirzek.

Imirzek, a small Turkish settlement in the Erevan district, on the right bank of the river Azat, in Mili canyon, is situated on the slope of a mountain.

The *in situ* ruins, consisting of the surviving lower portions of a wall of the church, are located at the center of the settlement, on a rock. Therefore, the fallen architectural fragments and inscriptions are not only scattered around the wall, along the fence of the church and on a floor, but also over the whole slope in the direction of the canyon, reaching even the channel which joins the river Azat.

Moreover, the local inhabitants have reused the ruins themselves for cattle sheds and the fallen fragments for building materials. Inscriptions, reliefs, ornaments and cross-stones (khachkars) have all been used for various constructions in the village.

The condition of the ruins and the scattering of the archaeological materials certainly complicated their study. With the help of an experienced worker brought from Ani, I immediately commenced my study of the ruins. However, I first had to solve the difficult problem of the fate of the constructions within the church itself and the nearby premises, which had been made from the stones and ruins of the church.

As a result of friendly conversations and my detailed explanations, the inhabitants and owners, who were initially unfriendly, started to sort through their constructions on the third day.

After this the work might have gone ahead faster, if not for the lack of workers. The local people, in spite of the fact that they were unoccupied, half-naked and hungry, agreed to work only rather reluctantly, evading daytime work because of the high temperature (they worked only before sunrise and after sunset), and esteeming their labour too highly. In addition, they at first appeared to be completely unusable for our work.

I was forced to ask for one more worker to be sent from Ani. Having then two experienced workers, I went ahead without any problem. In the meantime, the local people became familiar with our work and started to take part in it; occasionally up to 6-8 persons worked per day.

Working over 3 weeks, we completely cleared the church and the nearby areas to the west and north, where the cemetery was opened. We did not demolish the outside walls that now fence the church. The uncovered church-stones were assembled either in the church or on its western side. Many stones with inscriptions were found on the eastern and western slopes. When we were able to, we transferred them inside the same fencing.

The church, an elongated quadrangle in plan (Ya.I. Smirnov had measured it), is distinguished not so much by its size, but by its grace. It was constructed at the beginning of the XIIIth century, according to

---

* Delivered at the session of the Historical Philological Branch on January 16, 1913, and published in the *Bull. Acad. Impériale des Sciences de St.-Pétersbourg*, Série VI, 127, 1913.

the inscriptions. Irrespective of its size and grace, both typical features of a church, the abundance of the inscriptions (benefactions in the main), the splendor and beauty of the architectural finish, the richness and diversity of the ornaments and the numerous interesting reliefs, all point to the XIIIth century, the epoch of renaissance and flourishing of novel Armenian art. Of the reliefs, in addition to the figure of the builder in the attitude of prayer (costumed with stylized drapery), images of eagles (single-headed and double-headed), a peacock, a sphinx, dragons, etc. all attract attention.

The decorative engravings represent sockets, wickers and geometrical figures. Tiny ornaments also cover the plenteous cross-stones (khachkars). On the crosses themselves, the prevalence of pairs of circles on both ends of the wings was noticed. Not all reliefs are executed artfully ; there are rather rough images of people, of a horse, arms, etc. predominantly on funerary monuments of later epochs.

Almost all the stones possess the sign of the authors. Many of them, the larger ones, have handles for transportation. The latter are found mainly on grave-stones.

The number of assembled and read inscriptions exceeds 64 (four were found in the close vicinity of Imirzek).

All the Imirzek inscriptions concern first of all the local church. They contain the names of the heads of the monastery. In two stone fragments, lying far apart on opposite sides of the church, a very important inscription was found, mentioning constructions associated with a chair. The tombs of bishops were opened. Our first impression was that a bishop chair did exist in Imirzek. However, apparently, the inscription is about a chair or an outstandingly admired relic. The original name of the church (St. Virgin) has been discovered, and the ancient name of Imirzek (Vanstan) as well. Names of persons known from history, a number of geographical names, etc. are also mentioned. In the inscriptions there is an indication that one of the Imirzek figures was associated with building in Khor Virap. The Imirzek, or Vanstan, inscriptions, finally, have great palaeographical interest, especially due to the frequent use of wickers.

About 100 photographs, including general views of ruins and shots of architectural pieces, decorative details, reliefs and inscriptions, were made. All inscriptions are engraved on stones, except one written on the church wall in a pink paint. The majority of the inscriptions are from the XIIIth and XIVth centuries. To the latter epoch belong only the grave-stones ; no inscription of later than the XVIth century was found. One of the inscriptions from the vicinity of Imirzek, namely from Kyopri Kulakh, concerns the time of queen Khosrovanuysh (Xth century).

Noticing the growing interest of the local inhabitants in the archaeological finds, and their more sympathetic attitude to our work, I found it possible to ask three representatives of the population to undertake the care of the Imirzek monuments. They agreed with pride, due to my trust.

In the vicinity of Imirzek I examined other monuments, and their inscriptions were read and photographed. Work in Imirzek was terminated the evening of August 6. We returned via Geghard monastery.

II. REPORT PRESENTED BY A. KALANTAR AT THE ORIENTAL SECTION OF THE IMPERIAL RUSSIAN ARCHAEOLOGICAL SOCIETY [*]

Chaired by the Head of the Section, N.I. Veselovsky, the following fellow members and member-employees were present : N.G. Adontz, V.V. Bartold, V.N. Beneshevich, prince I.A. Javakhov, secretary I.Yu. Krachkovsky, N.Ya. Marr, A.L. Mironov, I.A. Orbeli, V.D. Smirnov, Ya.I. Smirnov.

Guests : Mrs.S. Davtyan and S.A. Loris-Kalantar, Mr.S.L. Gamalov-Churaev, I.A. Kipshidze, A.A. Loris-Kalantar, L.A. Smirnov, S.M. Shanshal.

A.A. Loris-Kalantar presented the report, illustrated by slides : "From the Trip to Yerevan State (Ruins of the Imirzek Church, Monuments of the Surmalu and Nakhijevan Districts)."

---

[*] Session of April 25, 1913. Published in the *Bull. Oriental Dept. of Imper. Archaeol. Society* 22, p. IX, 1914.

Last summer, in 1912, the lecturer made two trips to Erevan state, one to Imirzek at the behest of the Imperial Academy of Sciences, and the other to the Kurd-Ezides at the behest of the Ethnographic Department of the Russian Museum of the Emperor Alexander III.

The ruins of Imirzek (nowadays a small Turkish settlement) are situated in Erevan district on the right bank of the river Garni, in the Mili canyon. Study of the plentiful epigraphic material of the church of Imirzek, which had originally attracted the attention of Prof. N.Ya. Marr, was the main goal of the journey.

The church, of which only the bottoms of its walls have survived, was built on a high rock facing the canyon, so that fragments of the ruins are scattered over the whole slope and in the nearby canyons.

This circumstance, along with the fact that the local inhabitants have reused the ruins as sheds and the fallen fragments of the church as building material, very much complicated the study of the monuments.

With the help of two experienced workers from Ani, the lecturer succeeded during a three-week period to completely clear the site and open the ruins. All the architectural remains and inscriptions that surrounded the ruins were uncovered, and most of those scattered over the slope and in the canyon were assembled inside the church, on its western side, where they were surrounded by a wall.

The epigraphic material includes 64 inscriptions and provides new data on the site. All the inscriptions (of constructional, donation and memorial origin) relate first of all to the church. The most ancient of them — an inscription about the original construction — is attributed to 'the time of Atabek Ivane', i.e. not later than 1227. The builder was David — the spiritual leader of Ararat province. The name of the church, St. Virgin, and the ancient name of Imirzek, Vanstan, are also revealed. Figures known from the history of Armenia and Georgia, along with geographical names, are mentioned as well. In addition, the Imirzek inscriptions hold great palaeographic interest (due in particular to the frequent use of wickers) as well as a certain linguistic fascination (due to the manifestation of old Armenian language with dialects).

The architectural material gathered by the lecturer gives a clear image of the plan of the Imirzek church and the character of its decorations. The church, which is an elongated quadrangle in plan, is not large, but it is graceful. It is typical of XIIIth-century constructions — an epoch of revival and flourishing of novel Armenian art. By means of photos and slides the lecturer demonstrated to the audience the ruins and decorative details of the church, with its rich and beautiful architectural furnishings, variety of ornaments and many interesting reliefs. The reliefs, in addition to the figure in a praying pose in which the lecturer was inclined to see the builder of the church, David, include the figures of peacocks, a sphinx, dragons etc. The decorative engravings usually represent sockets, wickers and geometrical figures.

The Imirzek church provides data on the mutual relation of church and civil architecture. Moreover, concerning the question of cultural relations of the Christian Orient with the Muslim one, the new materials show that the processes in this part of Armenia were the same as in Ani (in view of the data of recent excavations there).

Discovered first in Ani, the front ornament of the altar of the church in the form of a decorative engraving is also observed here.

The next trip made by the lecturer, to the Ezides of Surmalu district of Erevan state, had mainly a ethnographic but partly also an archaeological goal. Briefly mentioning the results of his studies on ethnography, especially on the study of the religion of the Ezides, the lecturer presented materials on the ancient monuments of Surmalu and Nakhijevan, almost all of which were Armenian. He rescued many inscriptions of the Xth-XIIIth centuries and took numerous photos of the ruins of an ancient basilica in the village of Zor dating to the Vth-VIth centuries, an ancient caravanserai that he attributed to the XIIIth century, and fortresses.

In sum, the lecturer described the unhappy situation with the protection of archaeological monuments in the area, which he also illustrated with photos.

In the discussion of the report, the following individuals took part: N.Ya. Marr, prince I.A. Javakhov, V.D. Smirnov, S.M. Shanshal, I.A. Orbeli, and Ya.I. Smirnov.

III. THE EXCAVATIONS OF Prof. N. MARR AT ANI IN THE SUMMER OF 1910 *

Work during this summer commenced in early June: the first 20 days at "Main (*Boon*) Street," with simultaneous excavations in 5-6 different sites situated far from one another in various areas of the city. Obviously the excavations in these various sites will be crucial to a more efficient study of the city — of its constructions, cultural activity, and multi-side life — all of which are veiled by an opaque layer of uncertainty.

Starting on the eastern side, the first goal of excavations was the opening of the new entrance, which was totally obscured and at ground level. It is located in front of the St. Savior Church, atop the slope leading down to the Akhurian River. Of its walls and entrance towers only 1.5-2 m has survived. Presumably it was one of the main entrances of the city, as demonstrated by nice sculptural fragments in styles of various epoches, but having undergone so many repairs it was changed to such an extent that it finally lost its identity as a gate. This presumably happened as a result of the city's growth, when a new wall and a gate were built with the same orientation on the bank of Akhurian River.

No inscription was found that would allow the recovery of the original name of the gate, but due to its location, Professor Marr assumed that it was the Dvin Gate. Ancient historians had assumed that this was the name of the Chess Gate (due to its chess-like facade), which was located within the city wall and led to Galedzor, but this is completely wrong.

Excavations were conducted simultaneously at three sites along Main Street, which, as the key street of Ani, led from the Major (*Avag*) Gate to the Citadel (the Bagratuni's palace) along the length of the entire city, thus dividing it in two. The surviving minaret is situated on this street, and next to it is a building that we have used as a *hnadaran* (a storehouse for archaeological finds). To distinguish it from the newly built *hnadaran*, we call it the "Old Hnadaran" or the "Division of Hnadaran." The other, fallen minaret, and also the Abul-maamran Mosque and Square, are located almost at the mid-point of Main Street. Next on Main Street, towards the city wall, are located two hotels, which were partly excavated in 1908.

Obviously, the excavations on Main Street will have tremendous importance for the revealing of the architectural plan of the city due to connections with other streets and the fact that the entrances of the houses face the street.

These excavations began last year, when the section from the Old Hnadaran and Ashot's walls (opened during the excavations of 1893) up to the Citadel (i.e., the whole area of the Old City) was unearthed. This summer excavations were extended to the remaining sections of the street.

1. Starting at the Major Gate (i.e., at the top of the street), several stones with Armenian, Arabic, and Persian inscriptions were uncovered. Not far from the gate, in two places, stone stairs were unearthed (one with fallen stones), leading either to second floors or to roofs of houses. The floors of these houses, even their entire ground floors, were situated below the level of the road, which was walled along both sides, with these walls occasionally serving as the walls of adjacent constructions.

2. *From the Old Hnadaran to the Major Gate*. Here, near Ashot's walls, under a hill-like layer of the old street, human bones were found, partly burnt. A stone ball was found inside the remaining part of the skull. Near it were found several vessels containing mercury and a spear-point. The skull, judging from the form of the exposed cheek bone, was perhaps of Mongoloid type, although the curved nose bone seemed to contradict this.

The other two excavation areas on Main Street were located alongside the two hotels, towards the Major Gate and the minaret. On July 6 a water canal with clay tubes was uncovered in the first of these areas, at a very low depth. From the excavations carried out in previous years it was known that a canal passed along the entire length of Main Street as far as the Citadel's reservoir (cistern), which was unearthed in 1907. Therefore it was necessary to open the various sites along the street, in order to estimate the relative depth of the canal. The five opened sites showed that the canal became deeper over the total distance of 150 m between them, reaching a depth of 3.5 m at the final site. Its construction proved to be identical in the first four, namely with flat stones below and on both sides of clay tubes inserted one into another. All this was covered from above by a thick layer of clay and, again, flat stones. The tube was bigger than expected, and barrel-like (with the middle portions being thicker). The fifth site where the tube was unearthed was located between the hotel and the fallen minaret, where it was of a completely different type and extremely interesting. Here, on its western side, a strong stone wall over 3 m high serviced the

---

* *Horizon* 189, 192, 1910.

canal, which passed parallel to the wall. The stones of the wall were thoroughly smoothed, so that the upper stones had semi-tubular caving and corners that properly fitted one to another, giving the impression of a monolithic stone and forming a boat for the clay tubes inserted into it.

The city's water was transported via canals, which, judging from the historical chronicles, reached it from various regions and directions. These canals distributed water to various areas and constructions in the city. For example, the water source of the square "Miln i Modanis" and garrison buildings near the city walls, etc., are mentioned, as were the baths.

Clearly there were several water routes, since remnants of tubes were discovered several kilometers from the city, and they were oriented towards Ani. Thus the Sogyutlu source was by no means the only one to supply water to Ani.

Between the Main Street hotels and the Major Gate a square was opened, with the upper stones of the canal being level with the base of the square. It is remarkable that in this square, near the canal, a construction with nicely decorated niches exhibiting semi-pillars and arches was unearthed, and that its walls were properly built and its stones specially processed. All these were located about 2m below the canal. Although the existence of such a deep construction is remarkable, it is by no means surprising, since it was common for constructions in Ani to be repaired during subsequent epochs and hence to carry the signs of those epochs, and it was also often the case that new constructions were built on the top of older remains. I have to add that the upper stones of the canal mostly represent the remnants of various constructions, even one with an Armenian inscription:

ՈՂՈՐՄԵԱ

This evidence is beginning to confirm the claims found in ancient literary sources that Ani during its historical life underwent various big modifications. These are the markers of its various epochs, when a new culture developed upon the ruins of the previous one, thus adding more and more new layers to the city and clearly inspiring the ancient phrase "Ani is under the ground." These epochs are all very different, each with its own peculiarities.

During the period of prosperity of the kingdom everything was strong and solid, but later, under the Persians, a renaissance became necessary. This occurred during the time of Amirspasalars, when Ani reached the peak of its flourishing. Everything was gracious and beautiful at that time. However this also passed, its fame being replaced by misery, and with destruction rapidly approaching no one was able to maintain or rebuild anything. The continuation of life after the destruction is shown by the numerous fireplaces ("tonirs") that are spread over large areas of the city, giving rise to the name "fireplace epoch" for the period in question. This epoch continued right up to recent centuries and must have continued for a very long time, since the tremendous disruptions and damages that are evident in Old Ani cannot have been made within a short period.

Step by step the excavations are revealing this history, its every creation — the wall with its stone layers, the stones with their smoothed surfaces, the sculptures in all their various styles. The walls, these non-speaking historians, in their present pattern speak to us of every epoch, all of which have left their marks on them.

Thus, a stretch of Main Street nearly 600 m long was unearthed, with a smaller part still remaining.[1] Certain remains discovered during the excavations are of particular interest, therefore I will now mention them. The street, like the other sites, revealed numerous pots (mainly in pieces) that contained mercury. They were found especially in the vicinity of the hotels and the Old Hnadaran. These vessels were presumably decorations in all Ani houses. The mercury was kept in the pots, thus indicating the popularity of its use. The pots are egg-shaped, with squeezed edges, so that they could be either hung or inclined over another object. They had only a small hole in one side. They were presumably made of clay, but processed in such a way that they became as solid as the strongest stone, exhibiting a bluish-gray color in over ten shades. The pots are usually decorated on the exterior with rich bas-reliefs, but there are also some without decoration. The modeling shows seed-like elements of cereals, small crosses, stars, roses, sunflowers, other types of flowers, and even a female face. Most of the pots exhibit marks, although there are some without marks. Probably these are the marks of the potters. They may indicate also the size of the pot; and some of the pots are glazed.

---

[1] The excavations of the street and other areas were stopped due to a lack of resources.

Other interesting finds were the small pieces of pink stone that served to seal the clay vessels. They bear the images of a horse and a deer with a fawn, i.e., the scenes which were often found on the vessels. Near the hotel pieces of a glass vessel were found, colored in red and gold, including a fine picture of a fish. Also found was a complete round window of glass (the round shape being attained in the melting process). The surface is rough and modeled. This is remarkable, since window glass is known only from the XIVth century, while this piece, along with the other mentioned items, is from the XIIth century. Several remarkable pieces of decorated bricks with diverse figures were found as well.

The last site to be excavated was the Kars Gate. Located in the big city walls, on the northern side, near the Igadzor, this gate is still the highest and the most beautiful, with two standing towers. The portion of the gate situated between these towers is completely buried, so that its ruins form hills reaching almost half the height of the towers.

The hills were removed, the gate was opened, and what a scene! What an amazing mystery, a magical vision this gate is opening for us. It is impossible to describe it in a few lines. Every stone, every corner, every hole and cave has to be mentioned in order to show what harmony exists among them, and that together they form a gracious creation of military construction talent. From the outer side, the lower part only of the tower had survived, while the two towers on both sides of the gate had lost more than their half bulk. However these three-floor staired towers still carry on their facades the signs of the enemies' projectiles. Their covered roofs are decorated with arches, and their tops are connected by bridge-like spans. Below them is located the entrance, with traces of a double-sided door; and the lower parts of the walls are of unimaginable thickness. A door of monolithic stone closed the entrance to the lower floor of the tower. All in the past. But there is one more scene, a touching one: just by the entrance, on both sides, are the tombs of heroes who sacrificed their lives above upon the walls, who fell in defence of their motherland. They rest here to serve as examples of the heroism of the citizenry, as shown in the following inscription (of 1198) engraved in fine letters on a cross-stone:

Ի ԹՈՒ: ՈԽԷ: ԿԱՆԳՆԵՑԱՒ ԳԵՐԱՅՐԱՇ ՍՈՒՐԲ ՆՇԱՆՍ Ի
ԲԱՐԵԽԱՄՈՒԹԻՒՆ ՄԽԻԹԱՐԱ ՈՐԴԻՈ ԿԻՐԱԿՈՍԻ:
ՈՐՔ ԵՐԿՐՊԱԳԷՔ, ԹՈՂՈՒԹԻՒՆ ԽՆԴՐԵՑԷՔ Ի ՔՐԻՍՏՈՍԻ:

Ani, August 5, 1910.

GLOSSARY

by H. Melkonyan and G. Sarkissian

ADONTZ Nicholas (1871-1942) — Specialist of Byzantine and Armenian history, and linguist. Graduated from the University of St. Petersburg where he was a student of N. Marr. Author of the important study "Armenia in the Period of Justinian" and over 80 papers. Founded the chair of Armenology at the Catholic University of Leuven.

AGHJOTZ monastery — Mediaeval religious and educational center 12 km from Garni. Its surviving architectural monuments include the St. Stephanos and Peter-Paul churches (XIIth century), noteworthy for their graceful sculptures. Several remarkable manuscripts were written here.

AMIRSPASALAR — Highest military position in mediaeval Georgia and Armenia. Originated with Georgian king Vaghtang (1085-1125). Occupied initially by members of the Orbelian dynasty and since the late XIIth century by Zakarians.

ANI — Fortress of the Vth-IXth centuries, and later the capital of Armenia (Xth-XIth centuries). Important economic and cultural center situated in the district of Shirak, on the west bank of the river Akhuryan (today in Turkey). Ani had strong city-walls and richly decorated historical monuments. Its population numbered as many as 100.000 inhabitants. Ani became the capital of the Bagratuni kings of Armenia in 961. It was destroyed by the Seljuks in 1064, although it retained its economic importance as late as the XIVth century. In 1878 control of Ani passed to Russia and then in 1920 to Turkey. The site was excavated by N. Marr in 1892-1893 and 1904-1917, with the participation of A. Kalantar.

ATABEK — High official position in mediaeval Georgia and Armenia. In Georgia the position originated with queen Tamara (1184-1213). The first person to occupy it was Ivane Zakarian. Later it was occupied by Artzrunis.

BAGRATUNI — Ancient Armenian royal and prince dynasty. In the Vth century, members of the dynasty held positions as Armenian governors. From 885 to 1045, they were kings of Armenia.

ESAYI NCHETZI (1260/65-1338) — Teacher, historian, linguist. Rector of Gladzor University for many years. Had an active role in keeping the sovereignty of the Armenian church. The author of linguistic studies and manuals, lectures, and letters.

GARNI (Kotayk region of Armenia) — Ancient fortress believed to have been founded in the IInd century BC. In 59 AD Garni was destroyed by the Roman army; rebuilt by king Trdat I in the 70's AD. Later it was attacked by Persians, Arabs and Turks. Garni revealed monuments of various epochs: a Bronze Age dwelling, an Urartian cuneiform stone-inscription of king Argishti I, a temple of the Ist century AD, and mediaeval churches. The site was excavated by N. Marr in 1909 and by B. Arakelian in 1949. In the 70's the temple was reconstructed under the direction of A. Sahinian.

GEGHARD — Religious centre of mediaeval Armenia, a historical-architectural monument located 40 km from Yerevan. Also called "Ayrivank" because of a church in a hollowed-out cave within the rock. Presumably founded in the early IVth century but the surviving constructions are of the XIIth-XIIIth centuries and were built mainly by Proshians and Khaghbakians. Today it is an active monastery.

GLADZOR UNIVERSITY — Renowned cultural centre in mediaeval Armenia (1280-1340), situated in the Aghbertz monastery in the Vajotz Dzor region. Among the rectors of the university were several noted scholars, including Nerses Mshetzi, Esayi Nchetzi and Tiratur. Disciplines taught in the university included theology, philosophy, literature, music, arithmetic, geometry, logic, oratory, etc. Approximately 350 scholars graduated from the university. Patronized by the Proshyan and Orbelian houses.

GYOLAYSOR — Assyrian village located 20 km from Garni, presently in Khosrov National Park. Ruins of an ancient church and mediaeval tombs have survived. In 1920s the tombstone of queen Khosrovanuysh was taken to the cemetery of Gyolaysor (from the village of Khopri-Kulakh), where it was reused. Its inscription was first read by Ashkharbek Kalantar.

HARIJAVANK — Religious and cultural centre in mediaeval Armenia, situated in the village of Harij in the Shirak region. Its St. Grigor church was built in the VIIth century. In 1201 Zakarians built the main Kathogike church. The school of the monastery was active, with intermittent breaks, during the VIIth-XXth centuries.

HAVUTZ TAR — Mediaeval religious, cultural and educational center 5 km from Garni. Includes the St. Saviour church (XIth-XIIth centuries) and four others of the XIIIth and XVIIIth centuries. Suffered great damage during the powerful earthquake of 1679. A wooden picture of the crucifixion of Jesus, an important holy relic, was kept here (now in Echmiadzin). Numerous manuscripts were also written here.

HOVSEPIAN Garegin (1867-1952) — Art historian, Catholicos (Patriarch) of the Great House of Cilicia. Left a rich heritage of studies on various aspects of mediaeval Armenian history, manuscripts, fine art, architecture, epigraphy, etc. Participated in the excavations at Ani, Garni and Aragatz.

HOVNANNAVANK — Religious and cultural centre in mediaeval Armenia, situated in the village of Hovhannavan in the Aragatzotn region. Mentioned by historians from the Vth century on. Its oldest surviving building is a Vth century basilica. In 1216-1221, the prince Vache Vachutian carried out building operations in the main Kathoghike church.

KHAGHBAKIANS or PROSHYANS — Prince dynasty in mediaeval Armenia (Xth-XVIIth centuries). Originated in Artzakh. Its members played a major role in freeing Armenia from the Seljuk Turks, and were given additional regions for their victories. Were famous for their building activities.

KOBAYR monastery — Mediaeval Armenian religious centre with noteworthy pedagogical and cultural activity, situated in the Lori region of Armenia. Constructed in the XIIth-XIIIth centuries. Owned first by the Kyurikians and later passed to the Zakarians. Famous for its frescoes.

MARR Nicholas (1864-1934) — Orientalist, linguist and archaeologist. Member and vice-president of the Russian Academy of Sciences. Studied Armenian mediaeval authors such as Elishe, Eznik Koghpatzi, Mkhitar Gosh as well as the Georgian author Shota Rustaveli. Published numerous monographs and papers on the culture of Trans-Caucasian nations. Directed excavations in various regions of Armenia. Between 1892 and 1917, Marr headed the archaeological campaigns at Ani of which the results are summarized in his monograph "Ani" published in 1934. Organized the first (1916, Marr, Orbeli) and second (1917, Adontz, Kalantar) Van Expeditions. Founded the Academy of the History of Material Culture in St. Petersburg and the journals *Khristiansky Vostok* and *Bibliotheca Armena-Georgica*. Marr trained a number of outstanding scholars : N. Adontz, I. Javakhishvili, I. Orbeli, A. Kalantar, I. Meshchaninov, A. Shanidze, and others.

ORBELI Joseph (1887-1961) — Orientalist, historian, archaeologist; first President of the Armenian Academy of Sciences (1943-1947); Director of Hermitage Museum in Leningrad (1934-1951). Participated in the Ani archaeological campaigns (1906-1917). Visited and studied various monuments in western Armenia, including Aghtamar, Bagavan, and Bajazet (now in Turkey). Made ethnographic studies of Armenians and Kurds in Moks. Made fundamental contributions to the formulation of the scientific principles of Armenian epigraphy. Main publications include "Armenological Studies", "Corpus of Armenian Inscriptions - Ani", "Armenian Epos", and "Fables of Mediaeval Armenia".

ORBELIANS — Prince dynasty in mediaeval Armenia. Members played a fundamental role in XIIth-century Georgia, keeping e.g. the positions of amirspasalar. In 1211 they were important participants in the joint Armenian-Georgian army that freed Syunik. Later they had an active role in the political, military and cultural life of Armenia and were important builders.

GLOSSARY

ORBELIAN Stephanos (died in 1303) — Historian, metropolitan of Syunik Armenian State. Author of "History of Sisakan State", which covered in detail the political, religious and cultural events of the XIIth century.

PAHLAVUNIS — Prince dynasty in mediaeval Armenia that originated from the Arshakuni dynasty of Parthia. Moved to Armenia in the late IIIrd century. Grigor Lusavorich (the Illuminator), the first head of Armenian church, was from this house. There are no records about its members from the Vth-Xth centuries, but such records appear in the late Xth century, after which it soon became one of the influential houses of the Bagratuni kingdom. Members famous for their military, religious, building and cultural activities.

SARDURI II (died 735 BC) — The king of the kingdom of Urartu beginning in 764 BC. His activity is described in detail in the Van cuneiform inscription. Fought a war with Assyria in 753 BC and defeated six Assyrian kings.

SIMEON EREVANTZI (1710-1780) — Armenian catholicos (patriarch) beginning in 1763, historian, teacher, publisher of books. Founded the Echmiadzin printing house. Author of religious-historical essays. His chronicle "Jambr" contains the history of the Armenian church and descriptions of monuments.

STEPHANOS TARONATZI (ASOGHIK) — Armenian historian of the Xth-XIth centuries. Author of the "Universal History", which includes the history of Armenia from the creation up to 1004. An essential part of the book is devoted to the history of the Jews, Persians, Arabs and Georgians.

TEKOR TEMPLE — Located in the Shirak district of the Ayrarat State of Armenia (now in Turkey). Built by prince Sahak Kamsarakan in the Vth century. Contains the earliest mediaeval Armenian inscriptions. Destroyed in the earthquake of 1911 and studied by A. Kalantar.

VARDAPET — High religious degree in the Armenian Apostolic Church, held by heads of religious centres.

VOSTAN — District in Ayrarat State where the royal estates were situated. Two of ancient Armenian capitals, Artashat and Dvin, as well as the religious centre, were located here.

ZAKARIANS — Mediaeval Armenian prince dynasty (XIth-XIVth centuries). Members held important positions in the Georgian palace. They were commanders of the joint Armenian-Georgian army that freed Armenia from the Seljuks.

LIST OF PLATES

Pl. 1 to 14. The inscriptions from Vanstan and its vicinity. The numbers correspond to those of the manuscript.

Pl. 15. The church of Vanstan before the excavations (1912, photogr. by A. Kalantar).

Pl. 15 : 2 shows the members of the Vanstan expedition ; Kalantar is in the centre.

Pl. 16. Views of the excavated parts of the church.

Pl. 17. St. Virgin church : plan.

Pl. 18. St. Virgin church : eastern, western and northern facades.

Pl. 19. St. Virgin church : east-west cross-section.

Pl. 20. St. Virgin church : details of carved fragments.

Pl. 21-22. St. Virgin church : carved fragments uncovered during the excavations.

Pl. 23. 1-2. St. Virgin church : carved fragments uncovered during the excavations.

3. Sign of the master on the northern wall.

4. Khachkar (XVth-XVIth centuries).

Pl. 24. 1. Remains of a XIIIth century bridge on the river Azat in the vicinity of Vanstan.

2. The "Hieroglyph Stone" of Armavir in 1928. Kalantar is the second from the left.

Colour Plates (*in textu*)

Pl. I 1-2. The valley of the river Azat viewed from Vanstan.

3. General view of the monastery of Geghard.

Pl. II 4. Vanstan : St. Virgin church from the north-east.

5. Vanstan : St. Virgin church from the east.

6. Vanstan : the main facade of St. Virgin church.

Pl. III 7-8. Vanstan : Carved fragments.

9. Vanstan : frame of a window.

Pl. IV 10. Vanstan : fragment of the timpanum.

11. Vanstan : bas-relief with an eagle.

12. Vanstan : bas-relief from the church.

13. Khachkar of the XIIIth-XIVth centuries.

Pl. 1

1

2

3

Pl. 2

1

2

3

Pl. 3

1

2

3

4

Pl. 4

1

2

3

Pl. 5

1

2

3

Pl. 6

1

2

Pl. 7

Pl. 8

pl. 9

Pl. 10

Pl. 14

Pl. 13

Pl. 12

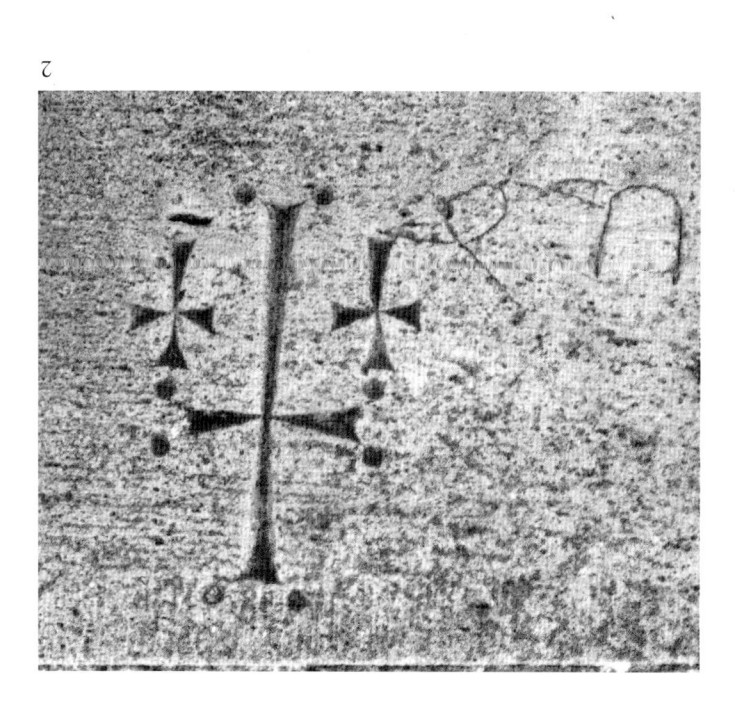

Pl. II

Pl. 15

Pl. 16

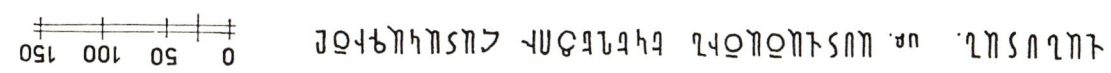

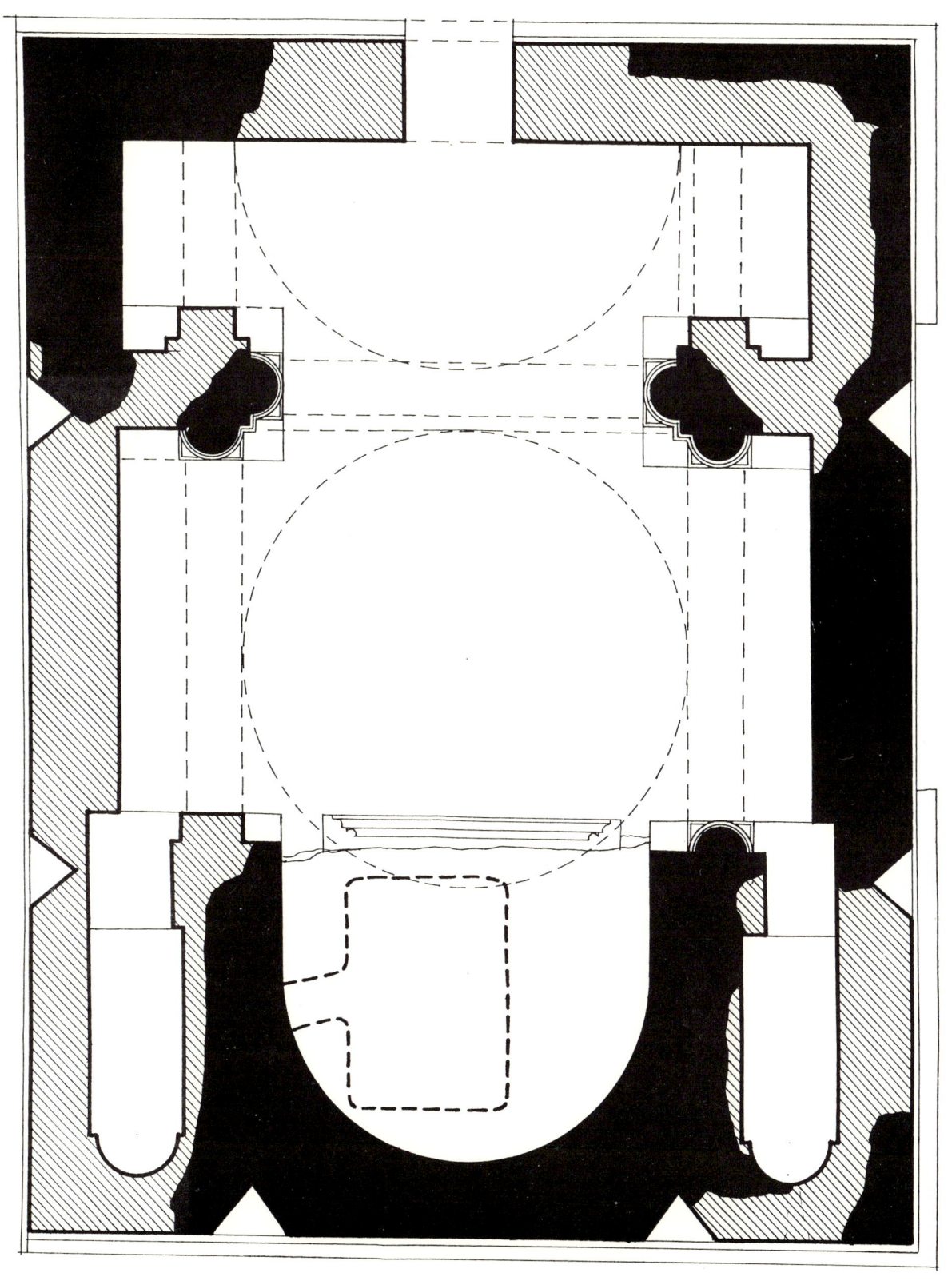

ՎԱՀՐԱՄ․ սբ․ ԱՍՏՎԱԾԱԾՆԻ ԵԿԵՂԵՑԻՆ ՊԵՂՈՒՄՆԵՐՈՒՄ ՀԱՅՏՆԱԳԻՐԸ

Pl. 18

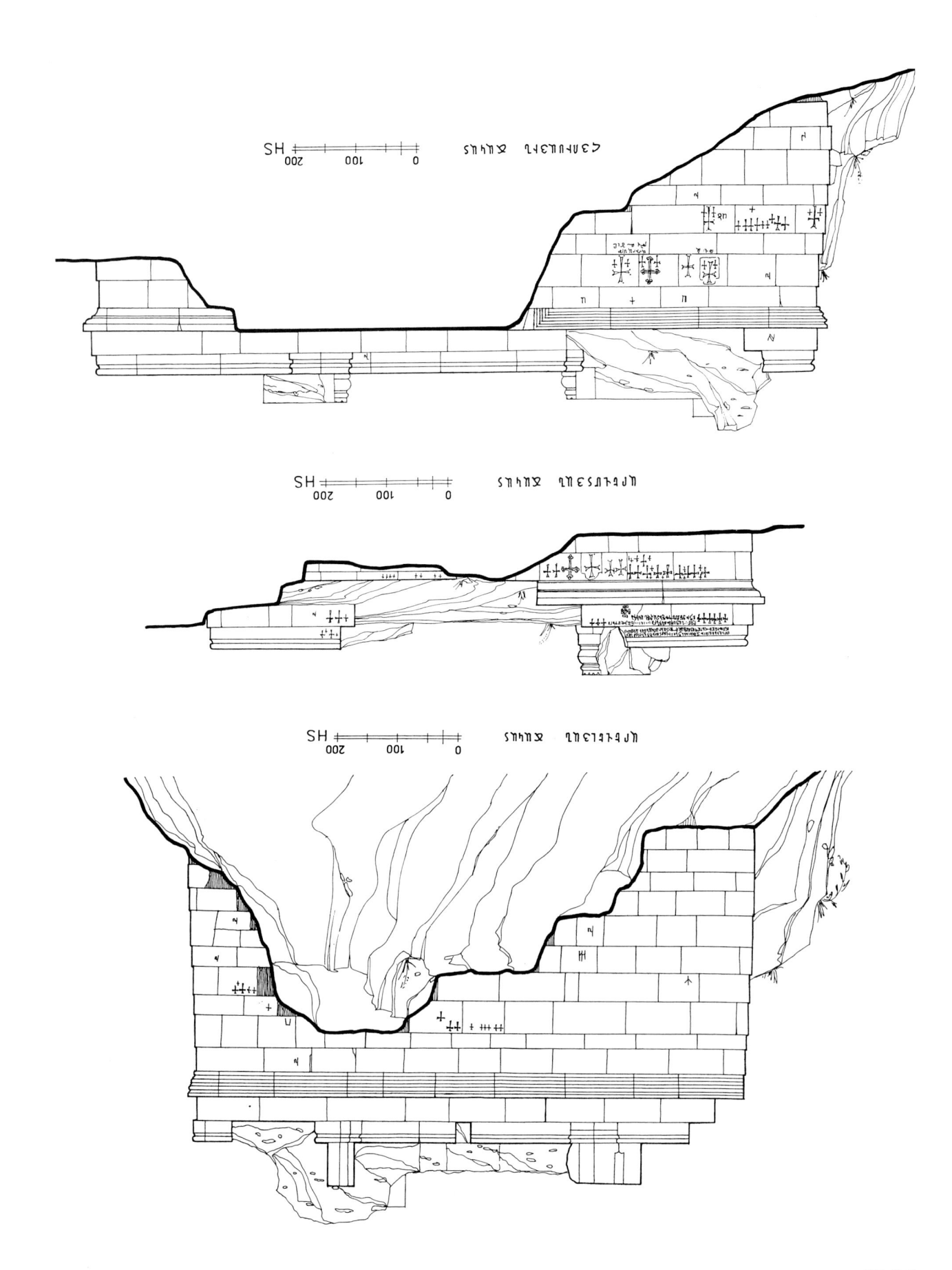

ԽԱՉՔԱՐԻ ԱՌԱՆՁՆԱԿԻ - ԱՐԵՎԵԼՔԻ ԱՌԱՆՑՔՈՎ ԿՏՐՎԱԾՔ

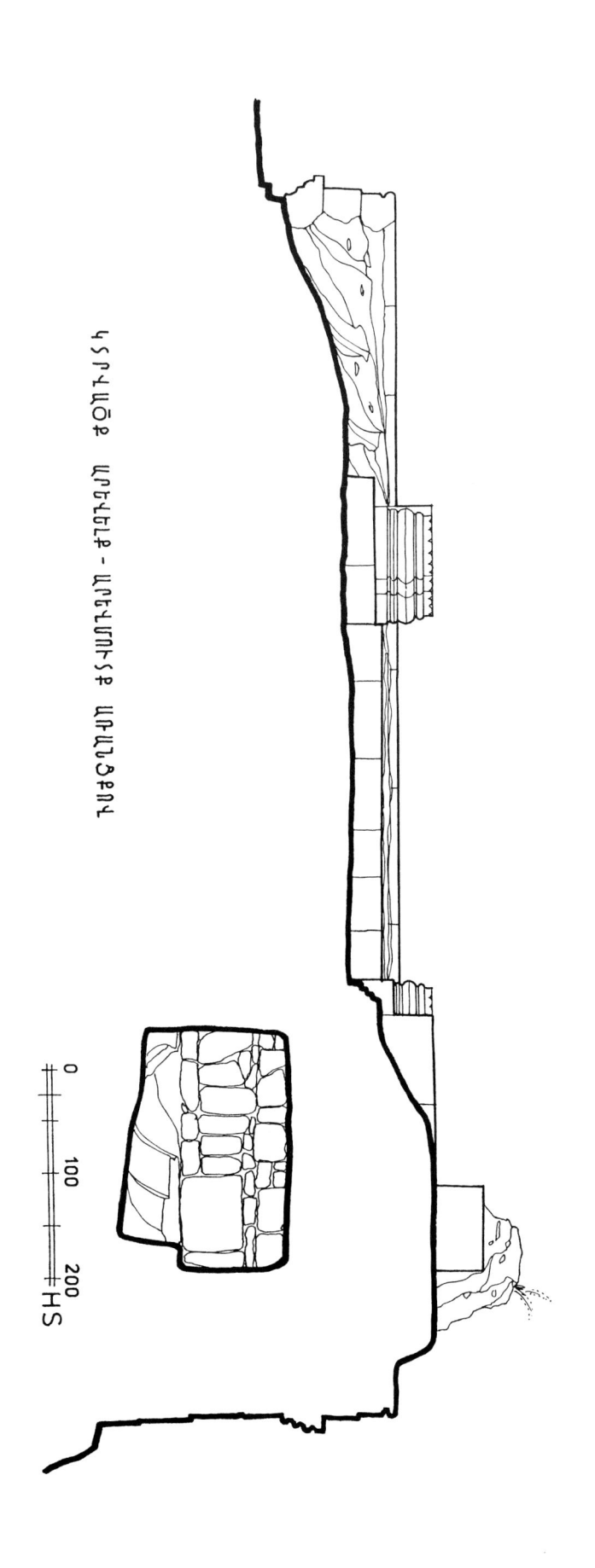

Pl. 20

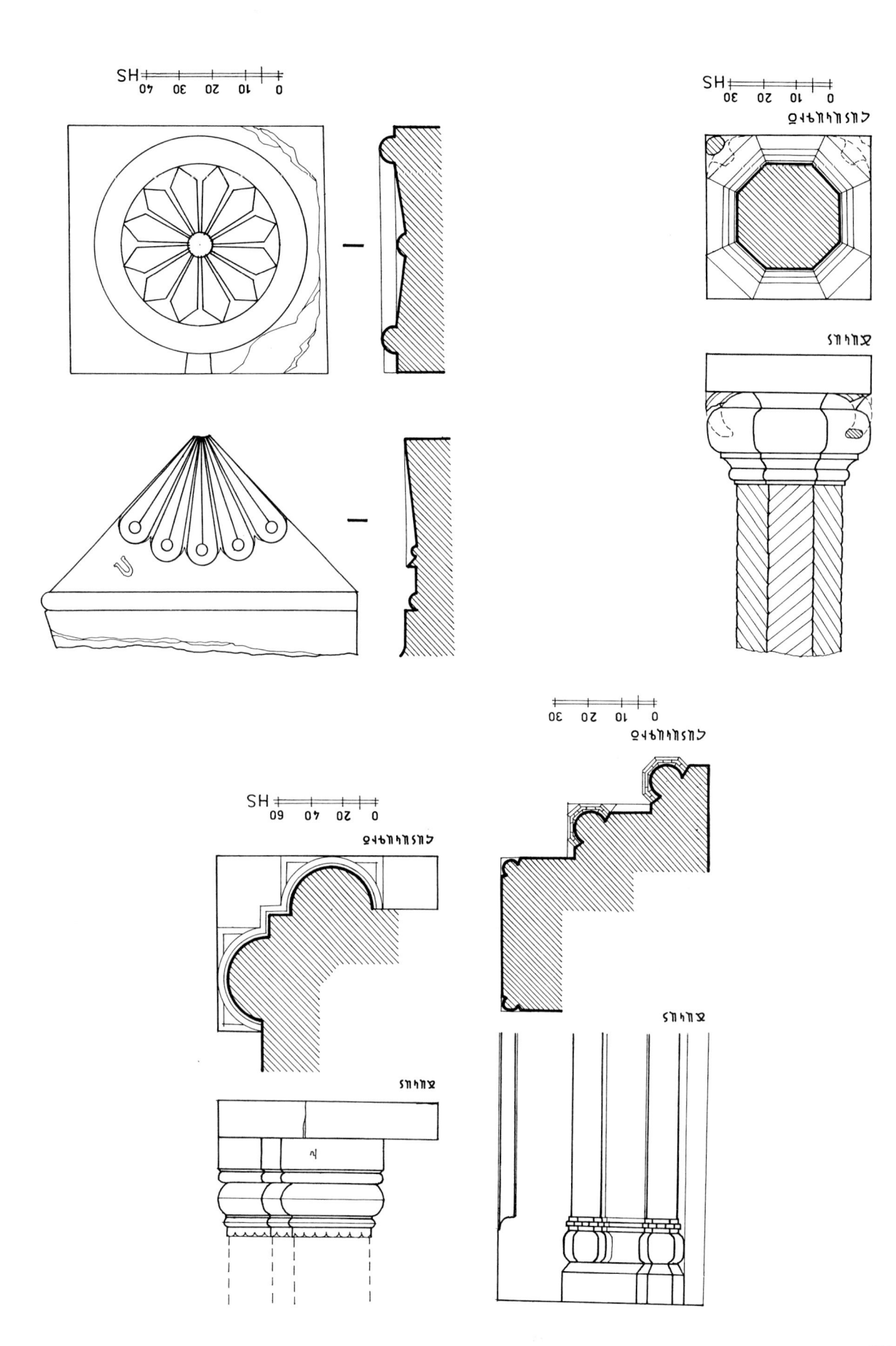

Pl. 21

Pl. 22

Pl. 23

Pl. 24